The Comedy of Evil on Shakespeare's Stage

Other books by Charlotte Spivack:

Early English Drama: From the Middle Ages to the Early Seventeenth Century (co-author)

George Chapman

The Comedy of Evil on Shakespeare's Stage

Charlotte Spivack

Rutherford • Madison • Teaneck
Fairleigh Dickinson University Press

London: Associated University Presses

Associated University Presses, Inc.
Cranbury, New Jersey 08512

Associated University Presses
Magdalen House
136–148 Tooley Street
London SE1 2TT, England

Library of Congress Cataloging in Publication Data

Spivack, Charlotte.
The comedy of evil on Shakespeare's stage.

Bibliography: p.
Includes index.
1. Shakespeare, William, 1564–1616–Religion and ethics. 2. Evil in literature. 3. Comic, The. 4. English drama–Early modern and Elizabethan, 1500–1600–History and criticism. 5. Moralities, English–History and criticism. I. Title.
PR3007.S66 822'.3'09353 77-69
ISBN 0-8386-2126-0

PRINTED IN THE UNITED STATES OF AMERICA

To my daughter, Carla
Laeta in Chorea Magna

Contents

Preface

Since my study of the comic representation of evil on Shakespeare's stage follows a long path through the centuries from St. Augustine to John Ford, it may be helpful to the reader if I explain my overall organization. The opening chapter, "Nothing and Iniquity," is concerned with the traditional Christian definition of evil as non-Being, ranging from Augustine to Aquinas and touching upon other church fathers along the way. In the second chapter I demonstrate how this definition led to the treatment of evil as a subject for comic derision in both the art and the literature of the Middle Ages. The comic vision of evil in medieval and early Renaissance drama occupies the third and fourth chapters, which survey the moralities and interludes. The comic depiction of evil in Shakespeare's own time is the subject of the last two chapters, where I consider first the plays of Shakespeare's contemporaries, then Shakespeare's own contribution to what had by then become a venerable convention of the English stage: the established union between comedy and iniquity.

I hope that the broad extent of my indebtedness to earlier scholars is at least implicit in the wide range of my footnotes. In addition I wish to express my profound obligation to a few individuals whose influence is beyond mere notation. To the late Hardin Craig I owe the love of rigorous scholarship in medieval and Renaissance studies, and to my teacher and friend William Bracy, the zesty discovery of those remarkable plays by Shakespeare's predecessors and contemporaries. To my doctoral student Meera Clark I owe much more than the careful labors of preparing the index, for her perceptive insights into Shakespeare have stimulated my own thinking about his plays. Above all, I owe a debt beyond words to my husband and fellow scholar, Bernard, by whom I was badgered, browbeaten, and buffaloed back into my original commitment to finish the book I had already begun, and away from the tempting distractions of new enterprises. I wish to thank Mathilde Finch for her energy and patience in dealing with this manuscript, particularly for her solution of thorny editorial problems wherever they occurred. I wish also to thank the editor of *The Cresset* for permission to use in my opening chapter material that originally appeared as an article in that journal. And finally, I should like to express my gratitude to the officers of the *Stefan Batory*, Polish Ocean Line, for their timely and generous offer of a typewriter.

Amherst, Mass.

The Comedy of Evil on Shakespeare's Stage

1
Nothing and Iniquity

"Malum est non ens"

1

THE association of evil and the comic is a commonplace in medieval art and letters. One immediately recalls the roaring demons in the eighth circle of the Inferno, the fire-cracking devils of the mysteries, and the incorrigibly grinning vices of the morality drama. Probably the most familiar symbol in the entire Middle Ages is the gargoyle, that grotesque figure of evil which leers mockingly from the sacred edifice of the cathedral. This remarkable association was perpetuated in the Renaissance, with the Elizabethan stage offering such diverse examples as Kyd's jesting scoundrel Pedringano, Marlowe's practical-joking devil Mephistophilis, and Shakespeare's smiling villain Richard III. And that this perpetuation was not merely theatrical is confirmed by a glance at the diabolic caricatures on the canvases of Bosch and Breughel. Such obvious examples are more readily observed than explained, however, and despite its familiarity (or perhaps because of it), this traditional union of comedy and evil has been accepted,[1] without scrutiny, as an adventitious phenomenon rather than as a significant one. But the unholy alliance of hell and humor had very deep roots: to the medieval and Renaissance mind it was not a superficial association of comedy and evil, but rather a profound philosophical conception of the comedy *of* evil.

The intimacy of laughter and evil in Christian art was no mere marriage of compatibles, but a genuine ideational consanguinity. For the comedy of evil in Christian art was the inevitable consequence of the definition of evil in Christian metaphysics. To elucidate the comedy of evil, then, it is necessary first to investigate this all-important definition of evil that remained remarkably constant from the origin of Christianity to its intellectual decline in the seventeenth century. From the patristic period through the Renaissance, the intellectual leaders of the church, whatever their speculative differences on other subjects, reveal impressive agreement on this one. It is this very agreement that uncomplicates the idea of evil in Christian metaphysics and qualifies the subject for succinct exposition through reference to the leading Fathers of the Church from Origen to Aquinas. The long history of this uniform interpretation of evil can therefore be readily summarized, and its implications for the comic portrayal of evil in art readily deduced.

In the third century after Christ, Origen, whose education under the combined tutelage of Clement and Plotinus prepared him for a philosophical synthesis of Christianity and Neoplatonism, formulated the definition of evil that was to survive him over a thousand years. According to Origen, evil has no reality but is defined precisely as the diminution or privation of reality. Evil has no essential being but exists only negatively, like darkness, which is in reality nothing but the absence of light. In short, evil is non-Being. This concept of unsubstantial evil was largely inspired by Plotinus, who had designated all Being as essentially good and attributed what seems to be evil to a lack of Being.[2] He had suggested that what is considered to be evil in existence is merely the privation of full existence; ironically, therefore, the negative "existence" of evil implies the possibility of greater positive good. In similarly denying the reality of evil and relegating it to the role of privation, Origen solved a problem that his mentor Plotinus did not face: he exonerated God from the onus of having created evil.

Throughout the early centuries of the Church, the Christian formulation of evil was challenged by the Manichaean doctrine of the eternal coexistence of equally substantial good and evil. The controversy involved no less than the fundamental conception of Deity, for the apostles of Mani believed in a Prince of Darkness who compelled equal recognition with the God of Light. Among those who for a time subscribed to this rational but pessimistic explanation of evil was Augustine. After wrestling for a long time with the paradox of evil in God's creation, Augustine finally resolved the tormenting dualism that seemed to threaten either the goodness or the omnipotence of the Creator. He rejected a Manichaean universe in uneasy equilibrium between equipollent principles of good and evil and subscribed to the belief of Origen that evil cannot *be*. In his *Confessions* he records his personal experience in reaching this new awareness:

> So we must conclude that if things are deprived of all good, they cease altogether to be; and this means that as long as they are, they are good. Therefore, whatever is, is good; and evil, the origin of which I was trying to find, is not a substance, because if it were a substance, it would be good. For either it would be an incorruptible substance

> of the supreme order of goodness, or it would be a corruptible substance which would not be corruptible unless it were good. So it became obvious to me that all that you made is good, and that there are no substances whatsoever that were not made by you. And because you did not make them all equal, each single thing is good and collectively they are very good, for our God made his whole creation *very good.*[3]

Later, in formal polemic against the Manichaeans, he developed further the notion of privative evil:

> Those things we call evil, then, are defects in good things, and quite incapable of existing in their own right outside good things. . . . But those very defects testify to the natural goodness of things. For what is evil by reason must obviously be good of its own nature. For a defect is something contrary in nature, something which damages the nature of a thing—and it can do so only by diminishing that thing's goodness. Evil therefore is nothing but the privation of good. And thus it can have no existence anywhere except in some good thing.[4]

The definition of evil as privation rather than substance continued to be expounded alike by Christians and Neoplatonists. The Neoplatonic Proclus (*On The Substance of Evil*) maintained the same position as his Christian contemporary Titus of Bostra (*Against the Manicheans*). Prudentius's *Origin of Sin* attested to the widespread acceptance of the idea among Latin writers and thinkers, while the works of such Greek fathers as Basil and John Chrysostom identified the concept with Christian theology as such. Basil echoed Augustine in his argument against the reality of evil:

> You must not look upon God as the author of the existence of evil, nor consider that evil has any substance in itself. For evil does not subsist as a living being does, nor can we set before our eyes any substantial essence thereof.

> For evil is the privation of good. . . . Now if evil is neither uncreated nor created by God, whence comes its nature? That evil exists no one living in the world will deny. What shall we say, then? That evil is not a living and animated entity, but a condition of the soul opposed to virtue, proce[e]ding from light-minded persons on account of their falling away from the good.[5]

By the fifth century the doctrine of privative evil had become a cardinal tenet in the expanding Christian theology, with the pseudo-Dionysius maintaining the position as follows (*Of Divine Names*):

> Evil does not exist at all. . . . Evil in its nature is neither a thing nor does it bring anything forth. . . . Evil does not exist at all and is neither good nor productive of good. . . . All things which are, by the very fact that they are, are good and come from good; but in so far as they are deprived of good, they are neither good nor do they exist. . . . That which has not existence will be nothing, unless it be thought of as subsisting in the good supraessentially. Good, then, as absolutely existing and as absolutely non-existing, will stand in the foremost highest place, while evil is neither that which exists nor that which does not exist.[6]

And in the sixth century, Boethius, although not a theologian and probably not even a Christian, advanced the privative nature of evil as a primary tenet of his *Consolation of Philosophy*. He suggested two consoling rationalizations that follow from recognition of the *privatio boni*. First, since evil as privation depends upon the good for its very being—or rather, its non-Being—then it must, as Augustine had already explained, ultimately destroy itself. "A thing exists which keeps its proper place and preserves its nature; but when anything falls away from its nature its existence too ceases for that lies in its nature." It follows, therefore, that even when the appearance of evil looms large, the apparent augmentation is actually a sign of imminent diminution and ultimate disappearance. The threats of even the most immediate evil can be dissipated through this recognition:

> You will say, "Evil men are capable of evil"; and that I would not deny. But this very power of theirs comes not from strength, but from weakness. They are capable of evil. . . . And this very power of ill shews the more plainly that their power is naught. For if, as we have agreed, evil is nothing, then, since they are only capable of evil, they are capable of nothing.[7]

No major theologian appeared between the time of Boethius and the Carolingian Renaissance. But before turning to the ninth century to resume the theme of evil as it recurs unchanged in the otherwise highly original Irish philosopher John Scotus Erigena, it is useful to make an important distinction. Without becoming involved in that favorite intellectual pastime of the Middle Ages—debating the problems of universals and the relationship of existence and essence—it is possible to clarify a point that may be ambiguous because of implicit assumptions about those very problems. In the above chronology of theoretical evil, the word *exists* appears in what seem to be two contradictory passages. When St. Basil declares "that evil exists no one living in the world today will deny," he seems to be refuting Dionysius's statement that "evil does not exist at all." As befits the subject of evil, however, what seems to be is not. The contradiction is only apparent, for evil does at once exist and not exist, depending on the meaning of the verb. This is to say, it exists experientially but not essentially, even as black exists to the senses only because real color is absent. In the metaphysical formulation of reality, evil is merely an appearance, not an *ens*.

This particular distinction—which is actually another way of denying the Manichaean dualism that attributed essence to both good and evil—was of major importance to Erigena, whose translation of the pseudo-Dionysius carried on the old reconciliation of Platonism and Christianity. He confirmed the definition of evil as non-Being: "Evil is nothing but the absence of God; matter is nothing but the absence of spirituality in the world"; and he elucidated the seeming existence of manifest evils as follows:

> They are good because God wills nothing bad; consequently there is no evil in nature. This does not prevent their appearing evil to persons who do not consider the whole of which they are parts, like the dark spots which contribute to the beauty of a whole picture. They are incorruptible because there is nothing evil to corrupt them. This does not prevent their freely willing irrational and illicit movements. (*Of the Divisions of Nature*) [8]

Three centuries later, the voice of the contentious Peter Abelard spoke out in uncharacteristic agreement with preceding and contemporary theologians on this one subject, the privative nature of evil. Abelard, who was also concerned with the impressive appearance of evil, concluded (*Know Thyself*) that this illusory threat is actually a desirable apparition in this imperfect worldly existence in that it serves as a test of Christian character: "Vice is a moral defect of mind, not inclining us to sin but providing the stuff of conflict which makes the triumph of virtue possible."[9] Like Milton, Abelard regarded the existence of evil as a necessary condition of active merit.

The fullest commentary on privative evil appeared in the thirteenth century in the massive *Summa* of Thomas of Aquinas. On this subject, as well as on almost any other relating to Christianity, the thinkers who come before St. Thomas subside into a prologue to him. Separated by a millennium of Christian thought and experience from the Platonic Augustine, the Aristotelian Doctor Angelicus agreed with the early African father on the privative nature of evil. Expounding the idea of deficient evil in greater detail than any of his predecessors, however, Aquinas first state the precept succinctly—"Malum est non ens" (Evil is no essence)—then developed it with characteristic thoroughness for the first time making a distinction between the non Being of evil as manifested in the physical and in the mora realms of creation. Of physical evil he stated simply tha "evil is the absence of the good which is natural and du to a thing. Nothing can be evil in its very essence."[10] Wh then is there such privation of Being, he goes on to ask why is there not complete good instead of varying degree of the absence of good? The answer lies in the very definitio of creation. "The perfection of the universe requires tha there should be inequality in things, so that every grade o goodness may be realized."[11] The physical evils of corruptio and death must necessarily characterize His creation, fo "God alone has the whole fullness of His Being in a manne which is one and simple, whereas every other thing has it proper fullness of being in a certain multiplicity."[12] God' universe is perfect because it is, in every way, a *plenum.*

As for moral evil, Thomas also denied its essence: "Every action has goodness in so far as it has Being; in so far as i is lacking in something that is due to its fullness of Being and thus it is said to be evil."[13] Again asking why, he reasoned that moral evil, unlike physical evil, is permitted rather than willed as part of the scheme of creation. Mora evil, therefore, has but an accidental cause. "[Moral] evi has no formal cause, but is rather a privation of form. So too, neither has it a final cause, but is rather a privation of order to the proper end. . . . Evil, however, has a cause by way of an agent, not directly, but accidentally."[14] He then added to his consideration of both kinds of evil an explanatory note to the effect that not every absence of good is evil "For absence of good can be taken in a privative and in a negative sense. Absence of good, taken negatively, is not evil; otherwise, it would follow that what does not exist is evil. . . . But the absence of good, taken in a privative sense, s an evil; as, for instance, the privation of sight is called blindness."[15] Thomas crystallized, from every possible point of view, the traditional dogma of nonessential evil. Bequeathed to him through a millennium of Christian assertion and amplification, it received from him so definitive and exhaustive a formulation that thereafter it faded as an explicit object of formal polemic and became instead an a priori assumption in Christian metaphysics. Even during the fourteenth-century storm of controversy over nominalism, the concept of evil as non-Being was not attacked, although the new school of Ockham challenged the prevailing concepts of Being. The privative nature of evil was to remain throughout the Renaissance a virtually unquestioned premise of the Christian world. Deeply ingrained in every Christian consciousness, the non-Being of evil functioned as more than mere theory; it became a point of departure for action, a basis for ethical choice. Primary expression of it occurred not in treatise but in deed, not in the cloister of speculation but in the arena of daily life. Before we examine its pervasive influence on the medieval mind, however, it is essential to review a corollary concept: the Chain of Being.

2

The Great Chain of Being was for both the Middle Ages and the Renaissance the accepted metaphor of the universal scheme of things. As a practical adjunct to theological doctrine, it constituted in effect a blueprint for the application of ideas, among them privative evil, to the created universe. As stated by its modern historiographer Arthur O. Lovejoy, the Chain of Being was

> the conception of the plan and structure of the world which, through the Middle Ages and down to the late eighteenth century, many philosophers, most men of science, and indeed most educated men, were to accept with-

> out question—the conception of the universe as a "Great Chain of Being," composed of an immense, or—by the strict but seldom rigorously applied logic of the principle of continuity—of an infinite number of links ranging in hierarchical order from the meagerest kind of existents, which barely escape non-existence, through "every possible" grade up to the *ens perfectissimum*—or, in a somewhat more orthodox version, to the highest possible kind of creature, between which and the Absolute Being the disparity was assumed to be infinite—every one of them differing from that immediately above and that immediately below it by the "least possible" degree of difference.[16]

Resulting ultimately from a combination of Platonic emanation and Aristotelian plenitude, the Chain had been endowed with a new perspective by its incorporation of Christian hierarchical values. The concept of the Chain had thereby become a moral as well as physical frame of reference. Because God at the top represented complete Being or goodness, it followed that the lowest orders of nature, those farthest removed from God, possessed not only the least Being but also the least goodness. Location on the scale was therefore qualitative: an angel is better than a beast because an angel has more Being than a beast. To the medieval mind, what was higher on the Chain was not merely different, it was better. Completely alien to the modern sentimental inclination to equalize all things—all God's creatures are equally wonderful, we say, as if they were wonderfully equal—is the constant value judgment exerted upon the physical universe by the medieval mind. Equally remote to the modern mind, with its secular values firmly rooted in the material world, is the medieval correlation of matter with evil. Although matter was not considered to be either wholly or substantially evil, the evil tendency of matter was a fact of central importance in the medieval view. Matter was considered less real than spirit. As Erigena defined it, matter is nothing but the absence of spirituality in the world. Mere matter, therefore, which was concentrated on the lower links of the Chain, was in itself a manifestation of the partial privation of being and as such identified with evil.

Since the doctrine of privative evil applied to the Chain of Being resulted in at least the association, though not the identification, of matter with evil and of spirit with goodness, the image of the Chain in its entirety provided for the medieval moral awareness a progressive lesson in *contemptus mundi*. Discrimination between good and evil began in the distinction between up and down. Consequently the moral implications of upward and downward thoughts and actions are present everywhere in the Middle Ages and Renaissance, even in casual mockery, as when Sir Philip Sidney condemns the man who does not like poetry for his "earth-creeping mind." And it was neither primitivism nor a fascination for the grotesque that led to the typical depiction of the devil as a beast. Satan conventionally appeared with animalized features—horns, tail, shaggy hair—embodying the animal passions and appetites that characterize the bestial aspect of privative evil associated with the lower orders on the Chain of Being.[17] To apply this double polarization of good and evil (absence of good) and of spirit and matter (absence of spirit) to human behavior, however, requires a careful look at the position of man on the Chain.

Man occupies a unique position, which endows him with unique attributes. Located exactly midway in the hierarchy of creation, man is the only creature incorporating all three orders of nature in one. As Dante, applying Aristotle, explains it:

> As man has been endowed with a threefold life, namely, vegetable, animal, and rational, he journeys along a threefold road; for in so far as he is vegetable he seeks for what is useful, wherein he is of like nature with plants; in so far as he is animal he seeks for that which is pleasurable, wherein he is of like nature with the brutes; in so far as

> he is rational he seeks for what is right—and in this h
> stands alone, or is a partaker of the nature of the angels.[1

As a result, man is a highly complex and also ambivalen creature. His remarkable situation affords him certain ex-traordinary advantages but also causes him quite paradoxica problems. Lovejoy describes the tragicomic ambivalence o this human "middle link":

> He is therefore—not in consequence of any accidental fal from innocence nor of any perverse machinations of evi spirits, but because of the requirements of the universa scheme of things—torn by conflicting desires and propen-sities; as a member of two orders of being at once, he wavers between both, and is not quite at home in either. . . . He is, in a sense in which no other link in the chain is, a strange hybrid monster; and if this gives him a certain pathetic sublimity, it also results in incon-gruities of feeling, inconsistencies of behavior, and dis-parities between his aspirations and his powers, which render him ridiculous.[19]

The most important attribute to follow from this trouble-some duality is moral freedom. In the phenomenal world, only man is endowed with freedom of choice; hence only man can move on the chain. Already participating in both the spiritual and material orders of creation, he can move toward greater participation in either. Already part angel and part beast, he can rise to more angelic stature to fulfill his spiritual aspiration, or he can degenerate to bestiality through surrender to his animal nature. Pico della Mirandola describes the possibilities in his *Oration on the Dignity of Man*:

> If you see one abandoned to his appetites crawling on the ground, it is a plant and not a man you see; if you see one blinded by the vain illusions of imagery, as it were of Calypso, and, softened by their gnawing allurement, de-livered over to his senses, it is a beast and not a man you

> see. If you see a philosopher determining all things by means of right reason, him you shall reverence; he is a heavenly being and not of this earth. If you see a pure contemplator, one unaware of the body and confined to the inner reaches of the mind, he is neither an earthly nor a heavenly being; he is a more reverend divinity vested with human flesh.[20]

From this viewpoint, man, free agent with a double nature, is also capable of two kinds of evil, physical and moral. Deprivation of his physical nature and deprivation of his moral nature are separate but analogous manifestations of non-Being in terms of human existence. Physical evil, for men, is bestial. It involves indulgence of the body, surrender to passion and impulse, a preoccupation with physical satisfaction at "the expense of spirit in a waste of shame." In short, it involves those sins which Dante punished in upper hell, such as lust, violence, and gluttony. In terms of the Chain, it means subordinating the superior to the inferior. Moral evil, on the other hand, is diabolic. It involves perversion of the intellect, distortion of that "right reason" by directing it to wrong ends, preoccupation with the unreal and the insubstantial at the expense of the real, the essential. It is the sin of Macbeth, who takes the witches' prophecy at face value.

In addition to the singular attribute of freedom, with its consequent possibilities for salvation or damnation, man possesses another unique trait: the capacity for laughter. Learned medieval treatises, exhibiting the typical fondness of the age for categorizing and classifying, defined man thus: *homo est substantia, animala, rationali, mortali, risus capax.* Like his freedom, man's laughter is also a result of his middle position on the Chain of Being. Man's comic perception is the direct result of his double view. Endowed with a perspective of his own incongruity, man is afforded laughter as a means of reconciling the contrary aspects of his dual nature. Directed downward from above, since the higher can comprehend the lower, laughter is the disdainful comment of the soul on the inferiority of the mortal, material body. To put it metaphysically, laughter is the response on the part of Being to the exposure of non-Being. In other words, then, laughter occurs when that which is real perceives the absence of reality, and when that which is good becomes aware of that absence of good which we call evil. As C. S. Lewis remarks in his *Preface to Paradise Lost*: "At that precise point where Satan meets something real, laughter *must* arise, just as steam must when water meets fire."[21]

3

It is at this point, then—"where Satan meets something real"—that the subject of evil becomes wedded to the mode of comedy. Laughter must arise at the perception of privative evil. To the medieval Christian who simply followed the definition of evil as non-Being through to its logical conclusion, laughter was actually inevitable. Taught that evil is not what it seems to be, that it is really nearest destruction when it seems most potent, that it is actually moving toward annihilation when it seems to be soaring with success, that it is literally approaching nothingness when it seems to be everything, medieval man could not do otherwise than laugh at the fundamental absurdity of evil.

To regard evil as an object of scornful laughter was not to take it lightly. To unmask evil and to penetrate its nature was, on the contrary, an operation of the utmost seriousness and laughter simply marked the triumph of recognition. Only by knowing the true nature of evil can one resist its misleading allure, and one's mockery of it, attesting this knowledge, attests as well his immunity. One can resist evil successfully only by seeing it as a shadow asserting substance, a nothing masquerading as something. It becomes a butt of humor to anyone who recognizes it as an impotent monster

hundering in a void. Puffed up in vainglorious insubstan-
iality, fuming with nonexistent prowess, promising equivo-
al rewards and veiling the eternal verities with temporal
rappings, the force of physical and moral evil becomes in
he light of immortal and all-encompassing goodness a
grotesquely comic thing.

The modern reader may object, however, that dismissing
evil as a joke, albeit good philosophy, is decidedly poor
psychology. Surely such a theoretical brushing aside of evi-
dent evils, while perhaps satisfying to the philosophical
mind, could not have meant anything to the untutored mind
of the ordinary man, even in the devout Middle Ages. Could
he theoretically privative nature of evil reduce the immedi-
acy of pests, pains, and plagues? Could the awareness of the
piritual non-Being of his wealth, his skin, or even his
physical life in any way comfort the robbed, the beaten, or
he dying? Surprising as it may sound today, the answers
could be affirmative even for the ordinary, pious medieval
mind. Just as it was possible for a Christian who really
anticipated a blissful eternity for his soul to regard life on
earth as a kind of "serio-comic interlude," as Henry Adams
put it, so it was possible for that Christian who really be-
ieved in the ultimate victory of the Good to see in evil only
a kind of seriocomic threat. Like Chaucer's Troilus, laughing
at the passions and pains of his life below on earth, he was
able to achieve a comic perspective on merely worldly woes.

Perhaps the modern reader's skepticism about the seem-
ngly naive psychological reaction of the medieval mind is
fostered by his recollection of Voltaire's devastating satire
on the "whatever is, is right" doctrine of the eighteenth
century. But the word *is* in this facile formula of Pope's does
not have the same meaning as the identical word in Augus-
ine's metaphysical postulation, "Whatever is, is good." If
"whatever is" refers to temporal, destructible, worldly things,
hen indeed to label everything "right" or "good" is a

rational absurdity. But if "whatever is" refers to the eterna
and incorruptible reality of spirit, then the denial of th
reality of evil is inescapable by Christian definition. Augus
tine's phrase is sound, for Being as such is always good. Bu
Pope's phrase, insofar as it refers to the multiplicity o
finite existence, does not really support but actually con
tradicts the theory of deficient evil. Because of the inter
vening change in concepts of reality between the Middl
Ages and the modern world, the two statements that soun
similar actually have meanings exactly opposed. To th
ordinary Christian of the Middle Ages, then, who believe
in the ultimate reality of the good, the best defense agains
the distracting illusion of evil was laughter. His laughte
was not at all naive, but a very practical defense based on
very deep faith.

Frequently, however, in what at first appears to be a per
verse dialectic, laughter issues not only from the witness o
evil but from the embodiment of evil. Actually, in thes
cases, two different orders of laughter are manifested, al
though both equally involve the illusoriness of evil. Th
characteristic humor attached to such demonic figures as th
mystery devils and the morality vices is not the intellectua
laughter of genuine superiority but rather the naive laughte
that rests on a deluded sense of superiority. The mocker
and gibes of evil characters are doubly funny in that the
only seem to be based on a comprehension of reality, wherea
they are but added reflections of deprived Being, of a limite
and distorted rationality. Milton's Satan, for example, be
comes more confident—and more comic—as he loses hi
grandeur and his power. Dramatically, this demonic laughte
combines with other conventional outbursts—usually copi
ous tears and rowdy anger—and in the plastic arts, wher
the pose is static rather than dynamic, the rigid grin is tha
of the absurd, the obscene, or the illusory. The comed
proceeding *from* evil, then, is but a confirmation and reflec
tion of the spectator's contempt *for* evil.

But how was the innocent spectator to recognize the nothing that was iniquity? By definition deceptive to the senses, might not evil become the genuine mocker instead of the mocked by eluding identification? How exactly could the tangible examples of this abstraction, *privative evil,* be isolated as proper objects of scorn for those who wished so to treat them? How can the belief that evil is non-Being enable men to penetrate the disguise of this manifest absence of the good sufficiently to permit the proper reaction of mockery?

The process of recognition was encouraged by the overwhelmingly sacramental view of life held in the Middle Ages. Aquinas had been struck by the fact that nothing man comes across explains itself, that nothing he encounters is self-explanatory: always everything depends on something else for its own intelligibility. In a world conceived of as a set of correspondences between things and ideas, everything finds meaning in reference to something apart from itself. For the mind oriented to the fourfold interpretation of Scripture, the leap from lofty ontology to pedestrian activity is not difficult. To one habituated to multileveled perceptions, a rose is not a rose and only a rose, but a rose is beauty that is also Mary and, as it often appears engraved on the tombs of early Christians, the figure of the soul's salvation. A man with this habit of thought readily illustrates his belief in the Trinity, like Browning's Spanish monk, by drinking his glass of watered orange pulp in three gulps. Another concept that aided the comic exposure of disguised evil was the speculum approach to reality,[22] which regarded the world as a moral mirror, with all particular things reflecting moral or religious ideas. With this habit of interpreting virtually every phenomenon as a lesson, the medieval mind sharpened its awareness of the many distorting mirrors of evil in the world.

The most important mirror of evil, however, is the aesthetic one. The individual psychological reaction to the perception of privative evil was multiplied and magnified in the universal artistic formulation of that reaction. Translated into art, the mockery of nonessential evil revealed its whole gamut of unreality from the bestial to the diabolic. Enacted in a thousand plays, reproduced in as many paintings, and built into every cathedral, the comedy of evil was scarcely less dominant than its austere sister theme, the Passion of Christ. The upward fervor of the sculptured saint and the downward grin of the gargoyle tell the whole story.

Notes to Chapter 1

1. In his recent study *The Play Called Corpus Christi* (Stanford, Calif., 1966), V. A. Kolve cites the affinity without exploring the reasons for it. Aspects of the subject have been touched upon by Willard Farnham, *The Medieval Heritage of Elizabethan Tragedy*, rev. ed. (Oxford, 1950); Willard Farnham, "Mediaeval Comic Spirit in the English Renaissance," *Joseph Quincy Adams: Memorial Studies* (Washington, D.C., 1948); A. P. Rossiter, *English Drama from the Early Times to the Elizabethans* (London, 1950); Helen Adolf, "On Medieval Laughter," *Speculum* 22 (1947): 251–53; J. S. Tatlock, "Medieval Laughter," *Speculum* 21 (1946): 289–94. None of the above investigates the comedy of evil as such.
2. See *Origen on First Principles*, ed. G. W. Butterworth (London, 1936).
3. Augustine, *Confessions*, trans. R. S. Pine-Coffin (Baltimore, Md., 1961), p. 148.
4. Augustine, "Contra adversarios legis et prophetarum," in *Patrologia Latina*, ed. Migne (Paris, 1886), 42, cols. 606–7. My translation.
5. "De Spiritu Sancto," *Patrologia Graeca*, ed. Migne (Paris, 1857), 29, col. 37. Cf. *Nine Homilies of the Hexaemeron* (Select Library of Nicene and Post-Nicene Fathers, 2d ser. 8), ed. Philip Schaff, trans. Blomfield Jacobson (New York, 1895): 61 f.
6. The quoted passage is translated by John Parker, *Works of Dionysius the Areopagite* (London, 1897–99), 1: 53 ff.
7. Boethius, *Consolation of Philosophy*, trans. W. V. Cooper (1902; reprint ed., London, 1940), p. 109.

8. The quoted passage is translated by George Bosworth Burch, *Early Medieval Philosophy* (New York, 1951), pp. 13–14.
9. Peter Abelard, "Scito Teipsum", trans. J. R. McCallum, *Abelard's Ethics* (Oxford, 1955).
10. Thomas Aquinas, selections from *Summa Theologica*, in *Basic Writings of St. Thomas Aquinas*, ed. A. Pegis, revised and corrected from the English Dominican translation attributed to Father Laurence Shapcote, O. P. (New York, 1945), 2 vols.
11. Ibid., Q. 48, art. 2.
12. Ibid., art. 1.
13. Ibid., Q. 18, art. 1.
14. Ibid., Q. 49, art. 1.
15. Ibid., Q. 48, art. 3.
16. Arthur O. Lovejoy, *The Great Chain of Being* (Cambridge, Mass., 1936), p. 59.
17. Ibid.
18. Dante, "De Vulgari Eloquentia," trans. A. G. Gerrers Howell, in *The Great Critics*, ed. James Smith and Edd Parks (New York, 1939), p. 140.
19. Lovejoy, *Great Chain*, p. 198.
20. Pico della Mirandola, "Oration on the Dignity of Man," trans. Elizabeth Livermore Forbes, in *The Renaissance Philosophy of Man* (Chicago, 1948), p. 226.
21. C. S. Lewis, *Preface to Paradise Lost* (New York, 1961), p. 95.
22. Walter J. Ong, "Wit and Mystery: A Revaluation in Medieval Latin Hymnody," *Speculum* 22 (1947): 310–41.

2

Demonic Humor in the Arts

"*My myrth is most of all.*"
-- Lucifer, *Towneley*, "Creation" 1. 96

1

TO the question of where we find the application in art of the comedy of evil, the answer must be: everywhere.

Comic representation of privative evil flourished in all the arts. United in a common homiletic purpose to project a common subject, the Christian arts consistently mocked the falsely strutting evils of this life—the lure of the senses, the threat of death, and the temptations of vice—by exposing the world, the flesh, and the devil as but shadowy negations of the eternal, the spiritual, and the good. In music, architecture, painting, and other arts, as well as in literature, the specters of death, decay, corruption, and damnation were grotesquely paraded for the moral edification of a population who might otherwise be deceived by such provocative illusions of Being.

The art of music was quite as allegorically conceived as was literature during the Middle Ages. Music was considered unique among the arts as the only one practiced in Heaven, and music was believed to be the measure of order in the universe. The planets moved rhythmically in a cosmic dance, and the harmony of the created world intimated the Divine. Man-made music, although inferior to the unheard music of the heavens, imitates the Divine order; consequently, the structural form and instrumentation of "musica mundana" had special significance.[1]

For example, the "perfect" rhythm, three-quarter time, allegorized the Trinity. Somewhat less obviously, the isorhythmic quartet allegorized human life, for, as in the conflict of appearance and reality in human experience, when one listens to this quartet, the rhythmic patterns that sound quite different to the ear are actually based on an identical numerical scheme, which is perceptible only through the intellect.[2] How does the comedy of evil as such come in for musical treatment? Three very different examples will illustrate it. First, the choice of instrumentation sets forth the idea. The psalter was used for sacred music, the cithara for secular. The psalter was believed to represent the spirit and the cithara the flesh simply because the music sounded from the upper part of the former instrument whereas in the latter instrument the sounds emerged from the lower part. Profane (hence evil) music and church music thus found their respective modes of performance in strict accordance with the chain of being, and the profane instruments played frivolous light music in the comic mode.[3]

Second, the existence of double liturgical texts also illustrates the inclusion of the comedy of evil in music for purposes of homiletic demonstration. Parallel Latin and vernacular texts were sometimes used together, the former for the sacred liturgy; the latter—with comic content—employed the reversed order of the melody proper to the setting of the former. These texts paralleled the double-plot structure later used in the drama, which poised a comic treatment of the theme in a subplot against the serious treatment in the main plot.

Third, since music was subject to corruption, attitudes toward music served as a means of characterization. A dislike of music was considered a sign of perverse will that rebelled against the divinely intended harmony. A character like Shylock, essentially a comic figure in the action, betrayed his evil nature by his rejection of music. In all of these instances, the projection of the symbolic comedy of evil into music, an art without moral content as such, particularly illustrates how deeply rooted and easily recognized this basic convention had become.

Similarly, the conventional mockery of evil played an essential role in architecture, which for the Middle Ages meant simply the cathedral. Art historians have stressed the significance of allegory in the study of church structure:

> Questions of the symbolical significance of the lay-out or of the parts of a structure are prominent; questions of its dedication to a particular Saint, and of the relation of its shape to a specific dedication or to a specific religious—not necessarily liturgical—purpose. The "content" of architecture seems to have been among the more important problems of mediaeval architectural theory; perhaps indeed it was its most important problem. The total of these questions would form the subject of an iconography of architecture.[4]

Even the orientation of the church building was allegorically meaningful.[5]

The great Gothic cathedrals of Europe, constructed as the architectural allegory, trope, and anagoge of man's literal existence, attempted to bridge the partial good of this life with the ultimate, everlasting good. While the vaulting spires strained heavenward, in lofty, precarious aspiration, the gutter drains spouted earthward through the gaping grins of gargoyles. And over the church portal were twin representations of the Last Judgment—the final alternatives facing every Christian. As for the explicit comedy of evil, it is present in at least four conventional forms in the cathedral.

Most familiar is the gargoyle, whose leering presence reminds the entering Christian that even while his soul seeks salvation within this structure, his body will pull him downward with the mocking demands of its physical being. But the fact that the gargoyles are also gutter drains—they are virtually always functional, rather than merely decorative—also reminds him that these physical processes are a necessary condition of this preparatory earthly span, and that they should therefore not be hidden or disguised but rather exploited as a symbol of mortality and blatantly scorned as that grotesque, inessential side of man's nature—which indeed they are. Their mockery is effective in forcing into proper perspective the lower physical processes of life. Whether they appear in a kind of visibly howling multitude, as they do, for example, in the cathedral at Dijon, or in glaring individual obscenity as in the cathedral of Freiburg, they can still make us see our animal selves and agree with Samuel Daniel that "vnlesse aboue himselfe he can/Erect himselfe, how poore a thing is man."[6]

Also facing the Christian as he enters the church is a second example of the comedy of evil. Over the front portal is a vast vision, usually divided into a double scene vertically and a triple one horizontally. God sits in judgment in the middle of the panel; on the left we see scenes of salvation and on the right scenes of damnation. The lowest tier shows life on earth, with the virtuous individuals quietly posed on the left while sinners disport themselves wildly on the right. The middle tier shows judgment day, with bodies arising from their tombs, already showing intimations of eternity, with the sinners amusingly gawking in fright or laughing in nervous misgiving. The top tier shows heaven and hell. On the left are rows of saved souls, who appear to a modern viewer rather smug and self-satisfied as they stiffly receive angelic congratulations. On the right is a very different scene: damnation is depicted as chaos and confusion, with shame and pain afflicting the poor, embarrassed, harried souls surrounded by boiling pots and sharp pitchforks in the threatening hands of grinning demons who thoroughly enjoy their work. One may ask—and, following the medieval mode of thought, one should ask—why is hell on the right? The answer has two parts. To be on God's right hand, the virtues must be placed on the entering worshipers' left, if the panel is to face outside. And the scenes are outside rather than within for a homiletic purpose (the church portal symbolizes the entrance upon the way to salvation): it is only knowledge of this way and entrance through it that can bring salvation. Fear of hell and hope of paradise bring in the faithful.

Inside the church two more conventional representations of the comedy of evil await the worshiper. One is of necessity rarely seen, but is none the less effective for that. In many Gothic cathedrals the contrasting portrayals of good and evil, of virtue and vice, take the form of parallel wood carvings in the choir stalls, where, suitably, the virtue is represented by carvings above the seats, often in the form of very exquisite figures of saints. But a matching set of representations of vice, showing workmanship of no less care and usually of considerably more imagination, presents itself *underneath* the choir stalls, the misericords, visible only when the seats are upturned. An excellent example of this bottoms-up comedy of evil in the choir loft is the striking group of misericords in the cathedral of St. Ours in Aosta. On each side of the choir, seven of the chair bottoms contain carved human figures engaged in bestiality or depravity of some sort. Perhaps representing the seven deadly sins, they include a glutton, a boy stealing from what appears to be a money bag, two children fighting over a stick, and, on one seat, the combined carvings of a death's-head and a jester, neatly epitomizing the union of comedy and evil! In addition to the human figures there are several carvings of animals eating prey, of grotesque monsters, and one of a monkey with his paw conspicuously placed on his outrageously uptilted rump. The cathedral of Toledo also has an artistically beautiful combination of good and evil panoramas in its choir loft. Virtue here assumes the form of a series of magnificent carvings of the Conquest of Granada, portraying the final triumph of Christianity over Mohammedanism. In contrapuntal relationship to this combat in a holy cause, a set of carvings directly below it also shows fighting scenes but of the opposite sort: animals tearing one another in struggle over bones, thieves squabbling over spoils, and so on. Altogether in this choir there are four tiers of the comedy of evil; in addition to the lower border just mentioned there are also carvings on the arms of the chairs and on posts dividing solid sections of chairs, as well as on the nether sides of the choir seats. Finely detailed and imaginatively conceived, all are effective, and some of the latter are particularly humorous in their caricature and grotesqueness.

Another somewhat less frequent example of the architectural comedy of evil is found in another part of the cathedral altogether: the pulpit. One of the most vivid examples of pulpit comedy is in the Cathedral of St. Stephen in Vienna. All along the curving stone balustrade of this huge and ornate pulpit, crawling upward in procession, are tiny beasts finely sculptured in stone: mice, frogs, lizards—some of the lowest and ugliest creatures on the chain of being. They are prevented from reaching the top of the railing by a dog that stands poised above them, threateningly holding back this grotesque parade. The dog, however, although above them, is himself not quite at the top. The priest, entering the pulpit after climbing along the railed stairway, stands above him as well. To mock these monstrous crawling figures, we need only to see the dog as the principle of higher ruling lower, and to laugh at both animal elements, we need only to infer the entire hierarchy of being, with the priest alone able to mount the pulpit. Once we understand this lesson in perspective, we can follow the advice of Boethius, confident that even climbing evil can never ascend very high.

The comedy of evil manifested in painting can help us to understand the otherwise puzzling canvases of Hieronymus Bosch.[7] On the strange canvases of this fifteenth-century artist, whom modern critics find surrealistic, the bizarre creatures in fantastic positions and arrangements represent, at least in part, the fifteenth-century version of the comedy of evil. Not so innocent as the merriment of the perhaps more confident thirteenth century, the comedy here is touched with horror, and the laughter that greets it is nervous rather than merely amused. But comedy it is, and the evil thus depicted in its deficiency is closely related to architectural gargoyles and stage devils. Bosch is a deeply religious painter, and his paintings are all designed for churches. His theme is always the conflict of good and evil, whether in the Temptation of St. Anthony, the scenes of the Last Judgment, or the "vanitas" representations of this world, the Haywain and the Garden of Earthly Delights. Probably his most obvious portrayal of the conflict is in the persons of the angels surrounding the lover in the Haywain triptych. The good angel is a properly Christmas-card figure, white, winged, and upward-looking. The evil angel is grotesque and clownish, with a sickening gray pallor, cymbal-shaped genitals, bat-winged, pot-bellied, and cloven-hoofed, with a snout ending in a long reed instrument that he deftly fingers while accompanying the lover on his lute. He seems to be crowned with thorns. Thus the profane music mockingly imitates the worldly lover's vain preoccupation, and the crown parodies, on the anagogical level, the Passion.

In most of his paintings, however, Bosch uses four devices for presenting the comedy of evil that are rather subtler in their allegorical content. Four of the puzzling items that appear in several paintings can be interpreted in exactly this way. The one that strikes the observer first is the frequently recurring "hollow shell" figure.[8] It assumes several forms: sometimes it is a hollow tree, sometimes an empty architectural ruin. These various shells yawn and gape, half revealing something evil, for example, a temptress lurking in the cavity of a tree trunk, a beaked monster peering from the eggshell: the temptation of illusion residing in what is essentially nothingness. The second thematic figure is the abortive growth—the tree that grows into a death's-head, the tower with weeds sprouting from its roof, a chapel overgrown with vegetation. These things are all thwarted in their growth toward Being, stifled into partial or non-Being, but again they usually contain or support some little, comic demonic figure. Third are the famous monsters that populate these remarkably detailed canvases. Most of them are freaks, men with duck's feet and bugle noses, apes with long beaks, a mouse the size of a horse, a cow with a pitcher for a rump, a bodiless head on two legs. They are obvious distortions or inversions of the proper order of Being. Finally, the cloacal close-ups that frequently appear resemble closely the gargoyles on cathedrals. Some, similar to one on the Freiburg cathedral, have the conspicuously upturned rear. Often, too, these anatomical items protrude from one of the hollow shells for further emphasis, in that the upper portion of the body is entirely hidden from view. The close-up may be a group of damned figures upside down, often with the upper half of their lowered bodies either obscured or combined with another scene.

That Bosch's strange world was not simply the product of his own fantasy is further confirmed by repetition of the same thematic material in the paintings of Breughel.[9] One aspect of the works of both men is the treatment of another manifestation of the comedy of evil which, however, found its most famous realization in a different artistic medium altogether, namely, the woodcut. The Dance of Death theme received its most complete, but by no means isolated, treatment in the woodcuts of Holbein.[10] The grim, but typically comic depiction of death served to comment on the vanity of transitory physical existence. In the Dance of Death scenes, the phenomenon of physical death is personified as a smiling skeleton, often in the attire of a professional jester, strumming a lute or dulcimer, laughing in diabolic glee as he waylays the unsuspecting victim: the vain woman at her toilet, the proud prince on his throne, the gloating miser in his counting room. Beneath the chilling effectiveness of the grim, bony hand of the fatal dancing partner is the challenging recognition that this is only a physical death. For death too is privative—life manqué, a skeleton without a soul.[11] Death's victims have made the error of putting their hopes and aims in this life. But if we know that death cannot take the soul, then the spectacle of the bones unclothed by spirit is a comic one. Thomas Sackville's description[12] of "the naked shape of man . . . All save the fleshe, the synowe, and the vayne" is frightening if we fail to recognize what Romeo called "insubstantial death." Then are we rather like Claudius in *Measure for Measure,* "death's fool." And it is the person busily engaged in worldly preoccupation who needs to be reminded through the medium of comedy that the flesh dies and the spirit lives. The scene of the gravediggers in *Hamlet* is but one of many scenes in Jacobean drama that portray the Dance of Death theme in a mood of mingled comedy and irony. The popular Jacobean convention of the "fatal revels"[13] is probably derived from the Dance of Death tradition as well. At any rate, that this device of a masque supposedly intended for entertainment suddenly metamorphosed into a literal death dance is a late and highly ironic manifestation of the medieval theme.

The comedy of evil infiltrated into ritual as well as art. The church itself had become early the scene of a ritualistic manifestation of the idea.[14] Certain festival days on the church calendar called for an inverted ritual, for example, Boy Bishop's Day, on which the holy hierarchy was overturned, with choir boys assuming the bishopric and bishops accordingly deposed and relegated to the choir loft. Similarly, on the Feast of Fools and the Asinarian Festival status was reversed, order replaced by disorder, Christian hymns travestied by vulgar dog-Latin verses, and even the official service parodied in secular language.

> Orientis partibus
> Adventavit asinus
> Pulcher et fortissimus
> Sarcinis aptissimus
> *Hez Ser Asne, Hez!*[15]

In short, the sacred gave way to the profane, but for the most sacred reasons. The obscene gestures and coarse language involved in these ceremonies, which evoked stern reproach even from contemporaneous church officials for their immoderation, seem unmitigatedly profane to the modern sensibility. But this paradox of sacred profanity and devout parody is another manifestation of the Negative Way of comedy applied to evil. The boy bishop indirectly confirmed the high holy office he falsely occupied; the ass ridden backwards down the church aisle indirectly confirmed the biblical account of the triumphant entry into Jerusalem; the inverted syllable of the mass indirectly confirmed the power of the proper formula; however, as inevitably happens on the popular, quite unintellectual level of practice, the concrete act having been initiated from a meaningful idea eventually became so interesting in itself as to obscure the theory that gave rise to it. Holy days always become holidays.

The stage manifestation of the comedy of evil also grew out of church ritual. But before we go on to investigate its presence first in the mystery cycles, then in more detail in the morality drama, it will be useful to note at least briefly its appearance in other forms of literature in the Middle Ages.

2

In literature—nondramatic as well as dramatic—the manifestations of the comedy of evil were diversified and widespread. They occur in both epic and romance, in both secular narrative and sacred vision. An early example is the eleventh-century French epic, *The Song of Roland,*[16] where the appearance of the heathen Saracens is each time heralded by their villainous laughter. The poet delights in this particular detail, making it explicit through repetition. The infidels, unjustifiably confident in their pagan strength, smile with glee as they march into battle against the ultimately victorious Christians, who, in their turn, appear always grave and pious as they carry on their holy war. As the "paynim" Marsilion's men report to him to discuss plans for Ganelon, each one laughs:

> Lo, now! there comes Paynim, Valdebron;
> He stands before the King Marsilion,
> And gaily laughing he says to Ganelon:
> (ll. 617–19)

Thereafter comes a Paynim, Climborin,
And laughing gaily to Ganelon begins:
(ll. 627–28)

Marsilion's nephew trips out before the throng,
Riding a mule which he whips with a wand;
He tells his uncle with laughter on his tongue:
(ll. 860–62)

Characteristically these evil figures swell with pride and boast in merriment as they foolishly strut to defeat by the forces of virtue.

In the thirteenth century the comedy of evil can be studied in its native setting, as it were, in scenes of Dante's *Inferno*. Critics have often commented on the broad farcical content of the 21st and 22d cantos in the first canticle of Dante's religious poem. Not at all incongruous, these cantos offer a typical example of the humor in art confined to the lower bodily functions, the bestiality in evil. When the grinning demons prod each other in the rump with their pitchforks, we are witnessing not only the disorder and chaotic disagreement that traditionally characterize the kingdom of the damned, but also the grotesque emphasis on what can only remain in the Inferno, where the good of the intellect has been irrevocably lost, that is, the beastly side of human nature. The devils whose "evil grin" frightens Dante bear animal names, translatable as Dogsnout, Dragonscowl, Tusker, Libbycocks.[17] As they relish their torture of the damned—"Just for fun, shall I tickle his rump for him?" "Nick him and prick him, boy—go on!"—their crude behavior betrays their own weakness along with the conventional obscenity that announced the fall of Satan in the mystery cycles:

They by the left bank wheeling chose their route;
But first in signal to their captain each

Thrust out his tongue; and, taking the salute,
He promptly made a bugle of his breech.[18]

Such demons are far removed in conception from the urbane, witty, and on the whole gentlemanly figure who appears as the devil in nineteenth- and twentieth-century literature. Stupid, ugly, and wholly bestial, these farcical demons are mocked beyond all possibility of awe or sly admiration.

In the fourteenth century, the vision of *Piers Plowman*[19] invokes the language of humor to describe the seven deadly sins. Each sin is depicted unsparingly as a physically weak and morally degraded creature capable of inspiring only pitiless mockery. Furthermore, in their shriving, these sins confess to laughter as characteristic of their own loose behavior. Pride scorns others, laughing loudly that ignorant men should deem her witty and wise. Even Envy admits "of mennes lesynge I laughe, that liketh myn herte" (B Passus 5, l. 112); Lechery takes pleasure in laughing at lecherous tales, and Gluttony imbibes with "laughyng and louryng" and "Let go the cuppe!" (B Passus 5, l. 344). Sloth had rather "here an harlotrie or a somer-game of souteres,/ Or lesynges to laughe at and belye my neighbore,/ than al that euere Marke made" (B Passus, ll. 413–15).

In the same century, another facet of the literary comedy of evil occurs, on a more sophisticated level, in Chaucer's *Troilus and Criseyde,* where mortality is appropriately mocked in the Christian context of faith and an afterlife. The hero, Troilus, at the end of the romance, can contemplate from above with ironic amusement the spectacle of his own worldly passions, now revealed in their non-Being:

And down from thennes faste he gan avyse
This litel spot of erthe, that with the se
Enbraced is, and fully gan despise
This wrecched world, and held al vanite
To respect of the pleyn felicite

That is in hevene above; and at the laste,
Ther he was slayn, his lokyng down he caste.
. . . .
And in hym self he lough right at the wo
Of hem that wepten for his deth so faste.[21]

The recognition of death's insubstantiality combined with the vision of this "wretched world" leaves Troilus in laughter.

The overt comedy of evil survives as late as the seventeenth century. A vivid example, written by T. M. and usually attributed to Middleton, not only reveals the tenacity of the convention but also relates it in specifically theatrical imagery. This particular work, satirical in purpose, is called *The Black Book.* At the beginning, Lucifer "ascends this dusty theatre of the world," revealing his plans:

Hence springs my damnèd joy; my tortur'd spleen
Melts into mirthful humour at this fate,
That heaven is hung so high, drawn up so far,
And made so fast, nail'd up with many a star;
And hell the very shop-board of the earth,
Where, when I cut out souls, I throw the shreds
And the white linings of a new-soil'd spirit,
Pawn'd to luxurious and adulterous merit.
. . . .
And now that I have vaulted up so high
Above the stage-rails of this earthen globe,
I must turn actor and join companies,
To share my comic sleek-ey'd villanies;
For I must weave a thousand ills in one,
To please my black and burnt affection.[22]

His performance will repeat a comic show of three centuries' standing. For what happens in nondramatic literature—from the grinning Saracens of the epic to the leering demons of the Inferno, from Langland's seven sneering sins to Middleton's comic and theatrical Lucifer—is but a fragmentary treatment of the theme compared to the major production of the comedy of evil in the drama. Let us turn initially, therefore, to the mysteries, the great cycles of biblical drama, in order to witness the birth of the theatrical prototype of comic evil.

3

The comedy of evil was an integral feature of the mystery plays, which evolved into cycles covering the entire biblical history from Creation to the Second Coming.[23] The comic element is appropriately initiated with the origin of evil—the fall from heaven. At the very moment of Lucifer's expulsion from the domain of God, a coarse jest introduces the theme of the privative nature of evil.

> Now to helle the wey I take
> in endeles peyn ther to be pyht.
> Ffor fere of fyre a fart I crake
> In helle donjoon myn dene is dyth.

(*Coventriae,* "Fall of Lucifer," ll. 79–82)

Also at that very moment Lucifer, and whatever fallen angels the particular play endows him with as companions, discover their blackness, that is, the absence of the light of goodness that had graced their heavenly appearance.[24] Lucifer thus remarks to Lightborn:

> We, that were angels so fare,
> and sat so hie aboue the ayere,
> Now ar' we waxen blak as any coyll
> and vgly, tatyrd as a foyll.

(*Towneley,* "The Creation," ll. 134–37)

Thereafter, whenever Satan or any of his fellow devils appear in the mysteries, a conventional comic formula identifies them: physical vulgarity, humorous howling, laughter, and vain boasting usually ending in tears of shame. For example, in the dramatized episode of the temptation in the wilderness, Diabolus, completely confident of success, blusters on stage, shouting:

> Make rome be-lyve, and late me gang,
> Who makis here all is thrang?
>
> (*York*, "Temptation of Jesus," ll. 1–2)

but a few lines later he staggers off humiliated, "Owte! I dar nozt loke, allas!" (l. 175). Again in the "Harrowing of Hell" play in the same cycle, he enters with a challenge: "What page is there that makes press,/ and callis hym kyng of vs in fere?" (ll. 125–26), but departs humiliated—"Nowe wex I woode oute of my witte" (l. 344)—and defeated, "Allas! for dole, and care,/ I synke in to helle pitte." (ll. 347–48)

Unsafe even in the nether kingdom, the devils reveal their characteristic weaknesses in the popular harrowing of hell episodes. Satan may at first appear defiant at the bold, determined knock at his gate by Jesus:

> Ffor all his fare I hym defy;
>
> . . . .
>
> And dyng that dastard downe.
>
> (*Towneley*, "Deliverance of Souls," ll. 161, 183)

He may even be able temporarily to reassure the terrified Ryald and Belzabub or similar cohorts. But he becomes himself an inevitable victim of the superior forces of virtue.

> Alas, for doy and care!
> I synk into hell pyt!
>
> (*Towneley*, "Deliverance of Souls," ll. 359–60)

And when in the Antichrist plays the devil is unveiled as an imposter, the lesson of deficient evil is most explicit. Actually powerless, though falsely commanding in appearance and manner, the figure is whisked off to hell "by the toppe" and "by the tayle."

Throughout the cycles it is not only Satan and the motley lot of fallen angels who are thus scorned. Wicked figures from biblical accounts are subjected to the same sort of mockery. Favorite butts of the comic routine were Herod and Pilate. The most notorious villain, and still well-remembered by the Elizabethans, was the ranting Herod. He boasts in much the same manner as had the proud, pre-fallen Lucifer:

> þer xal be neythey kayser nere kynge
> But that I xal hem down dynge
> lesse than he at my byddynge
>   be buxum to myn honde.

(*Coventriae,* "Massacre of the Innocents," ll. 138–41)

But he succumbs to the inevitable visitor, Death, who in turn can boast, "All thynge that is on grownd I welde at my wylle," and he is then seized by the rejoicing devil (*Coventriae,* "Death of Herod," l. 182) :

> All oure all oure this catel is myn
> I xall hem brynge on to my celle
> I xal hem teche pleys fyn
> and showe such myrthe as is in helle.

(*Coventriae,* "Death of Herod," ll. 233–36)

By no means limited to devils and villains, the deluge of scorn falls also on virtuous characters acting in the context of evil. Even such a revered figure as Joseph is not spared. At the moment when he begins to doubt Mary's chastity, he becomes that popular medieval figure of fun, the cuckold. He complains amusingly of his own impotence:

> I am old, sothly to say,
> passed I am all preuay play,
> The gams fro me ar gane.
>
> (*Towneley,* "The Annunciation," ll. 167–69)

Similarly, Noah remains a sober, virtuous character until his wife enters the play. Forced to do battle with his gossipy, tippling spouse in order to force her into the ark, he then becomes a hilarious, brawling, farcical figure. He pauses to warn the men of the audience:

> Yee men that has wifis whyls they ar yong,
> If ye luf youre lifis chastice thare tong.
>
> (*Towneley,* "Noah and the Ark," ll. 397–98)

As a further example, the shepherds in the nativity plays are allotted comic roles in their pre-sacred moments before actually stepping into the holy story. In the Chester cycle, after banqueting on "onyans, garlicke, and leickes," they fall to blows and stop short of carrying out their threat of breaking each other's bones only by the divine—hence serious—announcement of an angel that the miraculous star has appeared.

Noah's wife is but one example of the free invention of characters to embody the function of nonessential evil in the mystery plays. Further instances are Cain's boy, Mary's detractors, and various other servants, soldiers, and supernumeraries. As for Noah's wife, although she is named only once (*Towneley*), she always appears in the flood episodes, and her character is consistent throughout the cycles. She is distracted from her duty to her divinely chosen husband and from her opportunity to escape the deluge by her affec-

tion for her tavern friends and their boisterous pleasures
Her obstinacy and flippancy do more than serve to make
her a dramatic foil to her sensitive and godly husband. He
devotion to momentary physical pleasures reflects that dis
regard for spiritual values which is at the heart of the ver
evil that Noah has been chosen to refute by example:

> and let vs drinke or we depart,
> for often tymes we have done soe;
> for at a draught thou drinkes a quarte,
> and so will I doe, or I goe.
>
> (*Chester,* "The Deluge," ll. 229–32

The Towneley "Second Shepherd's Play" deserves specia
mention in this connection, in spite of its anthologica
familiarity, because the subplot involving Mak affords an
unusually complete example of the comic reversal of evil
The parodic scenes involving the theft of the sheep are a
clever inversion of the nativity narrative. The substitution
of the stolen sheep for the reportedly newborn child is a
farcical analogue of the divine birth of the lamb of God
As the shepherds stand about the poor cradle of Gill, the
shepherd's wife, waiting to honor her new infant, the man
ger scene is obviously paralleled. But when the shepherds
peep under the covers to do homage to the child, the sudden
revelation of the sheep's head is the hilarious exposure of
the true face of evil. Gill's excuse will not save her rascally
husband:

> he was takyn with an elfe,
> I saw it myself
> when the clok stroke twelf
> was he forshapyn.
>
> (*Towneley,* "Shepherd's Play" 2, ll. 616–19)

The deficient nature of evil has already been exposed. The

hepherd who almost gave Mak's "infant" a sixpence was leceived, but when he gives a bird to the holy child, he nows that the gift will bring him a blessing.

The mystery plays, then, demonstrated the first dramatic ise of the comedy of evil. Like the grotesque gargoyles on he cathedrals and the mocking distortion in sacred paintings, he so-called comic relief in this drama was not relief in he sense of balm for the tense nerves of spectators, but ather the bold bas-relief of evil exposed as laughable privaion against the solid background of the only reality, the good. The absurdly humorous devils and the realistic humor or episodes contrapuntal to scriptural narrative served a homiletic purpose by exploiting a habit of several centuries' standing: the habit of laughter at evil. The mockery of evil n the mystery cycles continually confirmed psychologically the definition of evil that had long ago been proposed philosophically: evil as non-Being deserves to be laughed at.

Notes to Chapter 2

1. See Manfred F. Bukofzer, "Speculative Thinking in Mediaeval Music," *Speculum* 17 (April 1942): 165–80; W. H. Auden, "Music and Shakespeare," in *Shakespeare Criticism, 1936–60*, ed. Anne Ridler (London, 1963), pp. 306–28; Frederic W. Sternfeld, *Music in Shakespearean Tragedy* (London, 1963).
2. Sections of music with the same underlying rhythmical pattern are called "isorhythmic periods" by modern writers. The abstract idea responsible for the pattern was based on the relation of rhythm to numbers and was comprehensible to the intellect alone. What the senses perceive as unrelated is unified only through the intellect, even as the multiplicity of human experience in life is unified only through the spirit. The form of the motet is thus a device for allegorizing the universe.
3. Ibid.
4. Richard Krautheimer, "Iconography of Mediaeval Architecture," *Journal of the Warburg Institute* 5 (1942): 1.
5. See Emile Male, *The Gothic Image*, trans. Dora Nussey (1913; reprint ed., New York, 1958). Male cites Gulielmus Durandus:

"The foundations must be disposed in such a manner that the head of the church lies exactly to the east, that is to the part of the sky in which the sun rises at the equinox" (p. 5). He goes on to explain that the north is consecrated to the Old Testament, the south to the New, and the western façade reserved for a representation of the Last Judgment.

6. Samuel Daniel, "To the Lady Margaret, Countess of Cumberland," in *Poems* (ll. 98–99), ed. Arthur Colby Sprague (Cambridge, Mass., 1939), p. 114.
7. See *Hieronymus Bosch,* ed. Carl Linfert (London, 1959).
8. Ibid.
9. See the discussion of Breughel in Otto Benesch, *The Art of the Renaissance in Northern Europe,* rev. ed. (Cambridge, Mass., 1965).
10. See Hans Holbein, *The Dance of Death* (New York, 1947). See also John Lydgate, *The Dance of Death,* ed. Florence Warren (Oxford, 1931).
11. It must be recalled, in this connection, that prostitutes at this time customarily wore a ring with a deathshead represented on it. Perhaps this custom is related to the notorious Elizabethan pun on "die."
12. Thomas Sackville, "Induction" in *Mirror for Magistrates,* ed. Lily B. Campbell (Cambridge, 1938; reprint ed. New York, 1960), ll. 384–85.
13. The convention occurs in *The Spanish Tragedy, The Revengers Tragedy, The Malcontent, Women Beware Women, The Broken Heart.* See Samuel Schoenbaum, "The Revenger's Tragedy: Jacobean Dance of Death," *Modern Language Quarterly* 15 (1954): 201–7; Theodore Spencer, *Death and Elizabethan Tragedy* (Cambridge, Mass., 1936).
14. A. P. Rossiter, *English Drama from the Early Times to the Elizabethans* (London, 1950) contains an account of this ritual of comedy.
15. Ibid., p. 58.
16. *The Song of Roland,* trans. Dorothy Sayers (London, 1957). Quoted are ll. 617–19 (stanza 48); ll. 627–28 (stanza 49); ll. 860–62 (stanza 69).
17. Sayers translation.
18. Dante, *The Divine Comedy,* trans. Dorothy Sayers (Harmondsworth, 1949). The quoted lines are translated from the *Hell,* canto 21, ll. 136–39.
19. William Langland, *Piers Plowman,* ed. W. W. Skeat (Oxford, 1886). Reprinted 1924.
20. Ibid.
21. Geoffrey Chaucer, *Troilus and Criseyde,* ed. R. K. Root, 2d ed.

(Princeton, N.J., 1926), bk. 5, ll. 1814–22.

22. Thomas Middleton, "The Black Book," in *Works*, ed. Alexander Dyce (London, 1840), 5:510.
23. Editions of the mystery cycles:

Chester Plays, ed. Hermann Deimling and J. Mathews (Oxford, 1892 and 1916)
Digby Plays, ed. F. J. Furnivall (Oxford, 1896)
Ludus Coventriae or *The Plaie Called Corpus Christi*, ed. K. S. Block (Oxford, 1922)
Towneley Plays, ed. George England and A. W. Pollard (Oxford, 1897)
York Plays, ed. Lucy Toulmin Smith (Oxford, 1885).

3

Morality and Mockery

I must nedes laugh; I can not be sadde.
-- Goods, in *Everyman*, l. 456

1

THE morality play, which probably originated during the fourteenth century, offers a microcosmic version of the macrocosmic material represented in the mystery cycles. It intensifies, in the person of a representative protagonist, the religious history of the human race recounted in the Scriptures. Rather than presenting episodes in the long life of mankind from creation to judgment, it abstracts the universal pattern of life common to all men and imposes it on an individual called Mankind or some other generic equivalent. Rather than rehearsing separate stories of the historic struggle of good and evil, it internalizes the conflict between these forces, locating it within the soul of the figure amed for the human race. The morality is the vehicle of a sychomachia, or spiritual conflict, in this case between hose impulses to good and evil present in every human eing. For the morality, therefore, the comedy of evil is not technique limited to the occasional appearance of an evil igure, as it was for the mysteries; not merely the "ensample f the bad" supplementing and highlighting the demonstra-ion of the good; the comedy of evil is the very basis of the norality play, inherent at once in its inception and its urpose. There are mysteries without evil, for example, the lays of Abraham and Isaac, but a morality without evil is contradiction in terms. By definition the morality must lemonstrate the nature of evil. Thus the particular nature nd development of the morality drama in England be-omes of central importance in a study of the comedy of evil, which found its proper vehicle in this genre.

Little is known about the beginnings of the morality play; nothing is known for certain about its exact origin.[1] What is definite is that its earliest extant prototypes ap-peared in England and date from the late-fourteenth and early-fifteenth centuries.[2] No logical predecessor exists from which to draw lines of continuity and development. Perhaps the Paternoster plays, which were performed in the four-teenth century, were the proper grandparents of the genre, but unfortunately there remain only scattered records of them and references to them. Otherwise, the nearest dramatic ancestors were the mysteries and miracles, both of which treat entirely different subject matter—biblical and hagio-graphical, respectively—in an entirely different way, both being literal representations rather than allegorical, at least in the modern sense of those words. The nondramatic relatives that treat the same theme, the abstracted conflict of good and evil, are distant in time and space. The theme actually goes all the way back to St. Paul, who contributed to Christianity—and, unwittingly, to the theater— a significant metaphor of the dualistic concept of man's nature and the inevitable conflict that results from it. Employing the imagery of battle, Paul bade the Christian gird himself to fight the forces of evil besieging him from within.[3] He saw in man a battleground for constant war between his inherent divinity, the spirit of God residing in his soul, and his innate depravity, lodged in the physical body condemned since the Fall. The concrete image of a battleground converted the moral dualism into a dramatic metaphor of life itself.

The conflict of these impulses to good and evil, that is, of the virtues and vices, received a fitting label and full literary expression in the fourth-century epic poem of Prudentius, the *Psychomachia,* where they are presented as personifications battling for eternal possession of the soul of man. There were at that time and in subsequent centuries many imitations of and variations on the military projection of the theme, with the result that poems and sermons often read like the journals of army generals, with doughty officers named Justice, Faith, and the like, opposed by forces with equally doughty but infinitely more deceptive officers, given to sabotage, spying, and dissimulation, and appropriately named Ill Will, Deceit, and so on. The twelfth-century *Anticlaudianus*, a didactic poem by Alanus de Insulis, surrounds the central figure of man with similarly personified virtues and vices; and the thirteenth-century French poem, *La Pélèrinage de la Vie Humaine* by de Guilleville generalizes and allegorizes human existence in terms of the same conflict within the frame of a pilgrimage. But although these and other works have the same theme and employ the same technique of personification, none of them is dramatic.

Something can be deduced, however, about the dramatic inauguration of this personified conflict from the study of extant moralities and of other literature and arts of the time, as well as of sermons that were concerned with the same theme, and the general historical atmosphere and philosophical temper. Theories have, in fact, been advanced as to the origins of the morality drama. Some scholars have accepted Prudentius as its founding father; some have favored the sermon as parent to this sermonizing play; some have considered it not as the product of any evolutionary process at all but as a distinct invention, the chance combination of allegory and the dramatic method.[4] Certainly as a new form it was not actually a novelty but rather a new combination of familiar elements—the Pauline metaphor of battle, the personification of vices and virtues as in Prudentius, the homiletic sermon, the tradition of allegorical poetry, and the religious drama of the pageant wagons. The moral play clothed an ancient metaphor in dramatic garb of homiletic materials tailored for popular presentation. But in any case, this is not the place to confirm, reject, or supplement these theories which, for lack of definite evidence, must for the time remain merely speculative. It is immediately relevant, however, for the sake of better understanding the distinctively English manifestation of this genre that successfully launched the comedy of evil on its dramatic career, to investigate certain factors closely involved with the beginnings of the morality: the highly eclectic and rapidly changing nature of the fourteenth and fifteenth centuries, particularly in England, and in that country the achievements of an English school of preaching and scriptural interpretation immediately prior to and during this era. Not merely transitional, in the general sense that every period is in fact a transition, these centuries were a time of genuine ferment, with the surfaces of the philosophical, artistic, political, and social terrains all erupting with innovation, rebellion, or reform. "Above all," comments one historian, "it is a time of eclecticism and shifting currents."[5]

In philosophy the great rebellion was nominalism. Set

forth by an Englishman, William of Ockham, the nom nalistic theory of universals challenged the Thomistic theor of their reality: with a devastating empiricism, Ockhar asserted the sole reality of individual things. The sovereignt of the individual left the universal as a mere sign by whic the mind represents reality to itself. "A universal is no anything real existing in a subject either inside or outsid the soul," he explains, "but anything which can be predicte of several things." Thus providing a purely psychologica explanation of universals, he completely obviates the inte lectual, speculative concern with the nature of essences, suc as God and the human soul.

In the church this new theological position had fa reaching results. An attempt to disengage faith and reaso succeeded the Thomistic reconciliation, and in effect na rowed the field of speculation for commentators: there wer no more "summas." Also in the church, along with th implicit beginnings of the Reformation in the latter pa of this century, and in support of or reaction to such reform popular preaching underwent a resurgence, particularly i England. Chaucer's parson, pardoner, and friar represen well-known types of the time. And along with the increas in preaching came an intensified emphasis on the *art* c preaching: the body of sermon literature surviving fror this period is not only voluminous but also often rich i literary variety and skill.

On the political and social fronts ferment and chang were no less characteristic. A series of peasant uprisings too place during these centuries, which also saw the emergenc of the secular state as an entity independent of the church Actually, the idea of a national state had been defended eve earlier by no less a Christian spokesman than Dante. An in the arts and sciences as well, the phenomenon of experi mentation occurs for the first time in centuries. In musi the Gregorian tradition is at last modified to make way fo

e *ars nova.*[7] And in science the works of Roger Bacon
d Robert of Grosseteste illustrate the awakening interest
the study of nature. It was to be, of course, another two
nturies before the study of science as such was born, and
is important to realize, in connection with all of these
tbursts in the direction of change, that they are only
eginnings. Mere cracks on the surface of the medieval
nthesis, many of these incipient rebellions fail to widen
sibly for at least another full century. Nothing changed
mpletely or at once, but for the first time in many hundred
ars, the auspices for change made its realization possible.
ften, however, it took the form of redirection or revitaliza-
on rather than revolt. The Protestant Reformation was
tended to be mere reform.

The revitalization of scriptural hermeneutics so dear to
e medieval mind is a case in point. To see what was hap-
ening to the four senses in scriptural interpretation, it is
ecessary to look back to the twelfth century, when Guibert
f Nogent made the startling proposal that since allegory—
e second sense—has fulfilled its purpose, it remains next
turn to tropology—the third sense—for further expatia-
on on the meaning of the scriptures. The new reign of the
opological, displacing in emphasis the typical, was briefly
itiated by Hugo of St. Victor, but awaited its real fulfill-
ent in England by Stephen Langton,[8] who inherited the
ictorine tradition from the French. Langton, working in
e ecclesiastical reform movement in England, was primar-
y concerned with a practical problem: he wanted to revive
nd invigorate preaching in England. Therefore he under-
ok to teach the art of effective preaching, but actually his
wo occupations merged. On the one hand, he engaged in
riting a commentary on the Scriptures, and what he wrote
as a continuous and independent commentary rather than
he traditionally inserted marginal and interlinear glosses.
n the other hand, he utilized these commentaries—

tropological in their aim and content—as preaching materia
He aimed at perfecting the technique of moralizing Scrip
tures for preaching purposes. To his students he recom
mended use of the tropological commentary—the "posti
lary," as it was called—as an exemplum in sermons. Sinc
the tropology indicated the moral lesson resident in a give
passage, it would serve, he said, as a "morality," thereb
giving the word its first recorded usage[9] as a literary tern
in English. Furthermore, as part of his clerical pedagogy
he recommended for his "morality" a mixture of element
grave and gay.

Langton's new methods had results. Aside from the popu
lar success of preaching to which his efforts contributed,
subtler effect ensued. The practice of the independent
tropological commentary was widely adopted and led even
tually to further separation of the Scriptures themselve
from the moral lectures ostensibly derived from them
gaining for the latter an autonomous force and validity
Detached from biblical content, they became extremely pop
ular in themselves. These sermons, with their detachabl
homiletic lessons, are concerned primarily with reformin
individuals rather than with positing universals, with illu
minating the conflict of good and evil within the Christian
soul rather than with demonstrating the historical conflic
enacted in the Bible. The spiritual successors of Langton
continued to employ the technique of personification en
livened with satirical detail, and, as a result, their sermon
make for interesting, even racy reading.[10]

At the same time, the mystery plays were dramatizing
literal biblical episodes with their typical, or allegorical
meaning either implied or rendered explicit in action and
dialogue. In succeeding centuries, these mysteries were to
decline in favor, particularly in England, where they also
achieved their greatest expansion. Having developed into
gigantic cyclic pageants, they eventually encountered in the
sixteenth century the stern opposition of the Protestant

eformation and suffered under Elizabeth the suppression
which their Catholic doctrine made them vulnerable.
hey aroused the antipathy of militant Protestants because
f their conservative Catholicism, and they stirred a more
niversal opposition because of their growing degeneracy.
The time was ripe for a new kind of religious drama and
he place particularly propitious for such a birth was
ngland. What appeared to supplant the mysteries and
niracles, to invigorate the Church's hold on the restless
opulace, was the morality play. Whether it actually origi-
ated in England is not known. But wherever it originated,
nd whether directly or indirectly from the "morality" ele-
nent in the sermon, the morality did appear as a separate
nd dramatic element, independent alike of a contextual
ermon or of a biblical text. And the moral play, as it ap-
eared, contained in its very nature—organically, not artifi-
ially—that mixture of grave and gay which Langton had
arlier recommended. For the content of that first moral
lay was the conflict of good and evil in the human soul
nd was probably first represented as the struggle between
he seven deadly sins and their corresponding virtues. And,
or the portrayal of the evil side in that war of personified
ices and virtues, the traditional definition of evil also sup-
lied a conventional technique of artistic projection. Al-
hough unchallenged in those changing times, the concept
f evil as non-Being stood in greater need than ever before
f support through the consoling retaliation of mockery.
The moral play from its inception adopted the method
waiting it from the pageant wagon and the sermon, from
he choir stalls and church portals, from altar paintings and
narginal drawings: the comedy of evil.

2

Before we investigate the early-morality manifestations of
the mockery of evil as such, it will be useful to establish

the particular nature of the English moral drama, for a
though we can only speculate as to whether or not the gen
actually originated in England, it did achieve a success an
fruition there that it did not elsewhere, and it also followe
a distinct pattern there different from that of so-calle
moralities elsewhere.[11] In fact, as will be demonstrated i
succeeding chapters, this particular pattern exerted a stron
formative influence over the Elizabethan drama that su
ceeded it. What enabled the English theater to achieve suc
a distinctive drama—so sharply different from, say, that c
the contemporaneous French stage—was the morality her
tage, a tradition too often slighted by modern scholarship.
For in England—as was not the case either in France c
anywhere else on the Continent—the morality play mai
tained a continuous, unbroken tradition for two centuri
—a tradition occasionally diluted but never really diverte
until the closing of the theaters in 1642. Those definin
features which became influential on later dramatic develo
ment can be deduced from the body of early English mor
plays.

The earliest of these extant moralities is the fragmentar
Pride of Life (ca. 1400).[13] The protagonist of this play
the King of Life, who defies his enemy Death, confident th
he can ward him off with the aid of his lieutenants, Healt
and Strength. But when through his witty, diverting me
senger, Mirth, he challenges Death to combat, the King c
Life is slain in the ensuing battle and his soul given ove
to waiting fiends. The prologue suggests, however, that i
the action that takes place in the missing final section, th
protagonist is saved from damnation through the mercifu
intercession of the Virgin Mary.

The earliest complete morality that survives is the *Castl
of Perseverance* (ca. 1425).[14] Here the protagonist calle
Humanum Genus is introduced on stage as a supposedl
newborn infant, but he matures almost instantly only t

ncounter temptation in the forms of the World, the Flesh, nd the Devil, each occupying a separate scaffold on the age. Led by a Bad Angel to the scaffold of the World, he elights in meeting there both Lust and Folly. Backbiter, erving as messenger for the World, next introduces his oung charge to Covetousness, who promptly summons ride, Wrath, and Envy from the scaffold of the Devil, and luttony, Lechery, and Sloth from that of Flesh. After emporary submission during his youth to these boisterous ins, Humanum Genus repents and is led by Shrift to the astle of Perseverance, where he is taken under the protec-ive custody of the seven virtues—Meekness, Charity, Absti-ence, Chastity, Industry, Generosity, and Patience. But the astle is forthwith besieged by the legions of evil. A rowdy ight ensues, with the virtues symbolically pelting back the oisy attackers with roses. In spite of the ignominious re-reat of the sins, however, Humanum Genus is lured outside y Covetousness, who has been inspired promptly to his ob of fresh seduction by a sound beating from his fellow ins. After a life of sinful self-indulgence, then, Humanum enus is at last struck by the irresistible dart of death, and alls in vain upon his friend the World to save him. After leath, his soul—crawling out from under the bed where e has been lying during the past 3,008 lines—is carried ff to hell on the back of the Bad Angel. But the Four Daughters of God—Mercy, Truth, Righteousness, and Peace —argue his case before God, who decides for mercy over ustice.

In *Wisdom Who Is Christ* (ca. 1461–75)—or *Mind, Will, nd Understanding,* as it is sometimes called—the center of he action is the soul of man, here called Anima. Together with its three faculties, the Mind, the Will, and the Under-standing, Anima is tempted away from devotion to virtue by the appeals of Lucifer in the guise of a gallant. But after a long depraved existence, displayed in a vaudevillian series of shows performed by the vices, he is eventually restored to the true way by the deeper persuasions of Wisdom Who Is Christ.

In *Mankind,*[16] written about the same time, the titular hero meets temptation in several forms. He is at first debauched by Mischief, who appears in the beginning scene to interrupt the long "predycacyon" of Mercy. Weakened by the wiles of Mischief, he subsequently falls easy prey to the trio of vices, Nought, Newguise, and Nowadays, who hold a mock trial to decide the issue of whether he shall receive from them a short jacket in the new mode. They also taunt him at his labor until he gives up the effort altogether. He then yields to the "fablys delusory" of the devil Titivillus, who leads him to further slothful neglect of his Christian duties. He interrupts his prayers to take care of a bodily need and he falls asleep, missing evensong. But Mankind is ultimately—and inevitably—reconverted. Saved from hanging himself in desperation by the patient, sententious exhortations of Mercy, he renounces the vices and recognizes the "net" that the devil had put before his eyes to delude him.

Everyman (ca. 1480),[17] the shortest of these early plays, is almost certainly Dutch in origin. Unlike the others in many ways, it concentrates on the summons of Death, with the result that it reads rather more like a final episode than a complete morality. The hero, Everyman, taken in hand by Death, finds himself deserted alike by his worldly friends, his physical powers, and his mental faculties. Only Good Deeds can accompany him to the grave.

Nature (ca. 1490),[18] written by Henry Medwall, posits the conflict of good and evil in terms of a struggle between reason and passion for mastery of the central character, Man. After spending several years in the sensual service of Mundus, Man recovers his reason and renounces his damnable worldliness.

The last of the early group of English moralities—*Mundus et Infans* (ca. 1510)[19]—traces the life story of a representative man by the device of name changes. Infans, whom his mother playfully named Dalliance, becomes Wanton at seven, Lust and Liking at fourteen, and Manhood at twenty-one. As he reaches the threshold of manhood, the World informs him of the existence of seven great "kings" from whom he may choose a favorite to serve. He quickly elects to follow Pride, who of course does not neglect to acquaint him with the other six members of his fellow royalty. Once in their grip, and encouraged by the vice Folly, he leads a debauched life in London that eventually qualifies him to be renamed Shame. When Conscience exposes and reviles the kings, who are in fact the seven deadly sins, he asks petulantly, anticipating the question to be asked of that later Puritan, Malvolio, "sholde I leue all game and gle?" (l. 449). After a long life of sin he is renamed Age, but, converted even at the very moment of impending death, he is permitted to expire under the name of Repentance.

The identifying characteristics of the earliest English moralities can be inferred from these briefly sketched examples. How these plays evolved will be considered briefly in the next chapter. The first distinguishing feature is the universalized concept of a protagonist. The central figure is always a typical, representative human being, generically named—for example, Mankind, Everyman, Humanum Genus—exemplifying if not all men at least all Christians. And from their inception these plays intended no less than full coverage of the whole life span of this generalized hero. With the exception of *Everyman,* the plays mentioned above are all full-scope moralities. The hero, like all men, is neither good nor bad but subjected throughout life to the conflicting impulses to good and evil within him. Pre-Calvinistic, he is permitted free choice between the paths to salvation and to damnation. For purposes of the plays, however, a different fatalism applies. It will be noticed that the universality of the protagonist determines his choice: mankind cannot be damned in a catholic homily intended as moral guidance toward salvation for the human race. A tragic outcome must await a later stage of morality development, when the hero has become *a* rather than *the* representative of the human race. Furthermore, as representative man the morality hero serves as a mirror of human behavior to the audience who were expected and explicitly instructed to see in this mirror the fatal alternatives resident in their souls.

Appertaining to the hero is the second characteristic feature, the theme of his dual nature. Every morality carries on the literary debate between the body and the soul, already popular in nondramatic form in the Middle Ages. *Mankind* makes a clear statement about this double human definition already discussed in connection with the Chain of Being:

> My name ys Mankynde. I have my composycyon
> Of a body and of a soull, of condycyon contrarye.
> Betwyxt them tweyn ys a grett dyvisyon;
> He that xulde be subjecte, now he hath the victory.
>
> Thys ys to me a lamentable story
> To se my flesch of my soull to have gouernance.
> Wher the goodewyff ys master, the goodeman may be sory.
>
> (ll. 194–200)

Humanity is necessarily a divided hero, and his divisiveness is displayed through the characters who surround him, for they personify the contrary impulses within his soul.

The third feature of the morality is its plot, which never varies. The undeviating action of every moral play is the Christian conflict between good and evil. The early moralities always present a full-length treatment of the moral sequence of events in man's life following his resolution of the inner conflict, or Psychomachia, between the good, which promises salvation, and the evil, which threatens damnation. Man, born innocent, encounters temptation in the attractive guise of vice; he is torn by conflicting impulses; his actions are the logical outcome of his choice between good and evil motivation; he dies and is divinely judged according to the ways he has chosen.[20] The sequence of cause and effect in his spiritual career dramatizes the static opposition of corresponding vices and virtues as expressed in Prudentius and other literary examples of this great theme.

Out of this sequence grows the fourth feature, which concerns the simultaneous internalization and externalization of the conflict. For the hero, the conflict is internal; for purposes of dramaturgy, however, the conflict is externalized in the form of personified abstractions. The subjective forces that in reality belong to man himself in the most personal sense are transformed by the poet into visible, external forces operating upon man. The Folly or Sensual Indulgence to which the mankind-hero submits is thus at once within and without; we see Mankind standing by helpless as his visible Conscience independently defends him against the visible vices who seek to enslave him. Obviously naturalism has no part in such a dramaturgy.

The fifth feature of moral drama involves this nonnaturalistic technique. Although modern readers are struck by the apparently "realistic" use of detail, particularly in later moralities, the moral drama is never realistic in the modern sense of "naturalistic." The moralities, actually dramatized moral homilies, are symbolic plays, and the essence of their dramaturgy is the symbolic use of action and language. Although more will be said about this feature in the context of particular plays, at the moment a couple of examples must suffice to clarify the point. The symbolic behavior of virtues and vices offers obvious examples. The virtues act in certain conventionally symbolic ways and speak in certain fashion; similarly, the vices inevitably perform certain characteristic actions and employ equally characteristic and symbolic language. For instance, the virtues speak proper, learned Latin; the vices indulge in a parodic pig-Latin. The virtues are always solemn and serious in demeanor and literal in meaning; the vices are boisterous and rowdy and their words are often equivocal. The virtues are clearly what they purport to be; the vices are frequently disguised. Nothing is more standard in the strategy of the vices than the deception they impose on their human victims through moral disguise, through, that is, their effective masquerade as a related virtue. This device, prescriptive for the morality plot, has considerable psychological validity as well: cowardice easily passes for caution, as Thucydides realized long before Christianity produced a moral play.

A sixth feature, also related to the symbolic dramaturgy, is the use of chorus and direct address to the audience. Characters step out of their stage milieu to inform or to warn or simply to joke with the members of the audience. In the *Castle of Perseverance* Titivillus pauses long enough from his seduction of Mankind to take up a collection from the audience! An interesting fact about these choral speeches is that their substance is always meant to be taken literally. The vice may be disguised successfully as far as the hero is concerned, but he reveals his true nature to the audience, whom he takes into his confidence in revealing, confessional asides. This homiletic technique of sincerity in soliloquy is later employed by Prince Hal, when he informs the audience of his intentions to reform before his actual behavior in the play encompasses this intention in any way.

The seventh feature, too, is a result of the symbolic nature of the drama. It is the comedy of evil, an innate and organic feature of the morality. Whereas in the mysteries comedy attached to evil figures whenever they appeared, and might therefore be lacking in plays without devils or villains, in the moralities evil plays an integral role. As there are no moral plays without vice, so there are none without the comedy of evil.

When Thomas Aquinas denied the substantial cause of moral evil, he explained that evil, however, has a cause by way of an agent, not directly but accidentally. Since evil is non-Being, then the role of the moral agent of evil must be comic by definition. For the moral agent of evil is but an accidental cause of nothing, of illusion. The function of the moral agent of evil in the moral drama is at first given over to scattered vices and only later concentrated on the Vice, who is therefore, throughout the stage history of the genre, a comic figure. His proper and original function demands that he be comic. The roaring devils of the cycle plays gave way to the lively, impudent vices of the morality plays, who cleverly tempt mankind to take his first step to damnation, and who pursue their machinations with diabolic glee. As the vices evolved into the Vice, the role became subtle, and his ingenious methods of seduction came to evoke laughter with as well as at him. Fundamentally, however, the dramatic function of the laughter fulfilled the homiletic purpose that the Vice personally delineated to the audience with pedagogical directness. His humor was rarely gratuitous.

3

The concept of evil as the absence of good not only authorized the mockery of evil but also implied the form that such mockery might assume. Since the homiletic aim in depicting privative evil was to scoff at its seeming substantiality, humor was directed at the discrepancy between its apparent Being and actual non-Being. This discrepancy was displayed in conventional behavior, which always characterized the role of vices and of the seven deadly sins. This behavior assumed three principal forms, pertaining to the respective privations of the world, the flesh, and the devil. First, the non-Being of the world is closely related to two prominent medieval Christian themes, Vanity and the Dance of Death. The vices teach their victims to behave with flippant disregard for the fact of death and the divine judgment to follow. They encourage devotion to the decaying flesh, the "dying animal" part of man, and attachment to the satisfactions of worldly life as such. Their victims, like Noah's wife, cling to worldly pleasures, wearing blinders in regard to the life to come, and, like Mankind, forsake their spiritual duty in favor of enjoying the "newguise" of "nowadays," which they forget is but "nought." The vices themselves, on the other hand, behave with an exaggerated and desperate fear of death as physical extinction, ironically asserting the very mortality that is the only permissible basis for their existence.

Second, the non-Being of the flesh is dramatized through emphasis on the physical grossness and weakness of the human body, particularly in its sexual and cloacal manifestations. Hence the vices in every way exaggerate the physical act, the negative or privative side of the nature of their human victims. And consequently, among themselves, they brawl in shameful physical violence, and joke in exceedingly obscene language about that behavior relegated to the lower half of man's body. They encourage lust and gluttony and take the greatest delight in diverting man from spiritual activity by urging physical indulgence. They become identified by their appetites, their grossness, their self-defeating sensual needs; but to their congenial human victims they become at the same time companionable chaps. This aspect of the role of Vice finally evolves into the appealing and amusing but quite unvirtuous "reverend vice" and "gray iniquity" of the Boarshead Tavern.

Finally, the non-Being of the devil is mainly demonstrated

through the complex theme of fraud. The vices always seem to be what they are not. They perform their deeds of seduction through perversion of language and action, through equivocation of all kinds, and through use of disguise. The devil is the father of lies, says St. John, and the vices, proper spawn of the devil, revel in falsehood. Liars in essence and in practice, then, they acquire considerable virtuosity in the fraudulent manipulation of the naive and trusting soul. Subtler than the outright lie is the equivocal use of language—words that seem to mean what they do not, prodigious promises that prove true to the ambiguous letter but false to the real spirit, like the prediction of the witches in *Macbeth*. They distract with blinding baubles of lesser Being from the clear light of total Being. As we are warned by Guazzo in his book[21] about the practice of black magic, the gold coins the devil rewards us with turn out to be merely gleaming pebbles. Disguise, too, is a necessary part of their equivocation, for the bare face of sin can frighten even those hardened sinners who have embraced its glamorously garmented exterior. The weapons—necessary for their warfare campaigns—are unreal. The vices wield an alarming collection of clattering insubstantiality—pots and pans, soup ladles, and brooms—and they explode firecrackers, frightening in sound but impotent to one who can see through the harmless smoke and futile din. They also parody Scripture and litany in similar-sounding sacrilege; they take mock oaths that tickle the ear with near conviction. And—above all—they laugh. Their laughter is that of coarse enjoyment in their dedicated work; they manifest joy in their own clever machinations. And at the point when we join their laughter, we are theirs. "The devil talketh with us wittilie. He eggeth us cunninglie. He deceiveth us craftily."[23] These privative evils reveal themselves comically in the early moralities already cited.

In the early, fragmentary *Pride of Life*, the comic figure

is called Mirth, the merry messenger in whom the King of Life falsely places confidence and who represents therefore the vain hope of mortals to laugh off death. He is always jolly:

> Madam, I make no tariyng
> With softe wordis mo;
> For I am Solas, I most singe
> Oueral qwher I go.
>
> (ll. 319–22)

Preoccupations with the light joys of this world—here personified—leave men unprepared for the next.

In the elaborate and prolix *Castle of Perseverance,* varied comic patterns symbolize evil in a range of forms. When the seven deadly sins, together with their mentors, the World, the Flesh, and the Devil, prepare to attack the Castle, stronghold of the virtues, they betray themselves by their brawling. World lambastes Covetousness, and Flesh flogs his lieutenants—Gluttony, Sloth, and Lechery—with Backbiter chuckling in diabolic amusement and unconcern at their misfortune. Meanwhile the devil Belial boasts and rages with amusing and vain fury, in the fashion of the mystery devils, complete with exploding gunpowder "in his handis, in his eris, and in his ers." Throughout, the vicelike messenger Backbiter plays gadfly to the World, Flesh, and Devil, with their more formidable energies, but as he enjoys the "good game" of the sins' humiliation, he also chuckles with approval and private delight, remembering his own "fals fame." The final separate defeats of the sins are by themselves humorously expressed as crude physical fiasco:

> Superbia: Out, my proude bak is bent! (l. 2199)
> Invidia: Al myn enmyte is not worth a fart. (l. 2208)
> Ira: I, Wrethe, may syngyn weleawo. (l. 2217)
> Gula: I do not worthe a the deuelys dyrt. (l. 2381)

Luxuria: For al my fere the qwene hath qwenchyd. (l. 2391)
Accidiė: I swone, I swete, I feynt, I drulle! (l. 2397)

Finally the Bad Angel gleefully scoops up his prey, the fallen Humanum Genus:

> Lo, synful tydynge,
> Boy, on thi bak I brynge.
> Spedely thou sprynge.
> Þi placebo I schal synge.
>
> To deuelys delle
> I shal tha bere to helle.
> I wyl not dwelle.
> Haue good day! I goo to helle!
>
> (ll. 3121–28)

The morality of *Wisdom Who Is Christ* presents evil for the last time focused in the form of Lucifer himself; hereafter, the role of seducer is to become more and more the prerogative of the Vice. But in this transitional play the devil, disguised as a gay gallant, remains the tempter. As he lovingly outlines his shrewd plan for enticing his victim, he explains his choice of disguise:

> For, to tempte man in my lyknes,
> Yt wolde brynge hym to grett feerfullnes,
> I wyll change me into bryghtnes,
> And so hym to-begyle.
>
> (ll. 373–76)

Marlowe's Doctor Faustus, asking the dark tempter to return as a Franciscan friar, learns this lesson directly. In attractive guise, the Lucifer of this morality easily persuades the faculties of Will, Mind, and Understanding to surrender to his sensual diversions:

Lewe yowr stodyes, thow ben dywyn;
Yowr prayers, yowr penance, of ipocryttys the syne,
Ande lede a comun lyff.
What synne ys in met, in ale, in wyn?
What synne ys in ryches, in clothynge fyne?
All thynge Gode ordenyde to man to inclyne.
Lewe yowr nyse chastyte and take a wyff.

(ll. 470–476)

And Will cheerfully submits to this temptation, blithely conceding

Met and drynke and ease, I aske no mare,
Ande a praty wenche, to se here bare.
I reke but lytyll be sche mayde or wyffe.

(ll. 814–16)

Once under the influence of Lucifer, then, the hitherto solemn faculties become themselves comic figures, subject to the same mockery as he insofar as their submission to him deprives them of their proper fullness of Being.

The somewhat later morality of *Mankind* is so full of coarse humor that it long elicited a charge of degeneracy from scholars who failed to recognize the homiletic intention of its large-scale comedy of evil. But Mark Eccles's introduction to his recent edition of the Macro Moralities acknowledges the success of its "high-spirited fun." The amusing mockers and tempters play a necessary role. "The author had a serious purpose, to warn men against the world and the Devil, but in achieving his purpose he made use of lively humour and of comic action" (p. xliii). *Mankind* is rich in the symbolic action of privative evil, in which the obscenities play an important part. In this play the mockery of evil is directed particularly against the vice of "newness"

—the moral agent working in the service of the World. As the play opens, Mischief mocks the long-winded "predycacyon" of Mercy, parodying his pious pedantry and learned Latin with the usual pig-Latin of vice:

> Corn seruit bredibus, chaffe horsibus, straw fyrybusque.
>
> (l. 57)

The trio of vices, Nought, Newguise, and Nowadays—representing that desire for novelty which springs from over-attachment to worldly things—embody the evil of that desire in their profane and earthly behavior, which is by no means merely what Pollard calls mere "horseplay and elemental dirt." Their actions in good part serve as obvious commentary on Mankind's own speech on dualism, which ends with a castigation of the body:

> Alasse, what was thi fortune and thi chaunce
> To be assocyat wyth my flesch, that stynkyng dungehyll?
>
> (ll. 203–4)

When Mankind has recognized that the flesh is but a "stynkyng dungehyll," the coarse, cloacal Christmas song of the vices comments on the temporary victory of the dunghill side of Mankind's nature:

> Yt ys wretyn wyth a colle, yt ys wretyn wyth a colle,
> He that schytyth wyth hys hoyll, he that schytyth wyth hys hoyll,
> But he wype hys ars clen, but he wyppe hys ars clen,
> On hys breche yt xall be sen, on hys breche yt xall be sen.
>
> (ll. 335–42)

Crude, to be sure, the song is nonetheless relevant thematically. Later in the play Mankind neglects his prayers in favor of attending to such a bodily need, politely excusing himself for the purpose to the audience:

> I wyll into thi yerde, souerens, and cum ageyn son.
> For drede of the colyke and eke of the ston
> I wyll go do that nedys must be don.
>
> (ll. 561–63)

This coarse song, which anticipates Mankind's degeneration, is often omitted, along with similar passages, by modern editors who do not recognize their homiletic purposes. The Christians of the fifteenth and sixteenth centuries did not expect euphemisms to conceal the appalling nature of that loss of Being which they knew to be evil. Just as they did not neglect the overt horror of bones and worms in their portrayal of death, they did not slight the overt vulgarity that they associated with privative evil.

A further example of such symbolic humor in the play is the mock court scene. The facetious trial carried out by Mischief and the three vices centers on the theme of newness. The object of the court judgment is a new-fashioned short jacket, and to win it Mankind is willing to accept a series of commitments to sinful existence, prescribed by the vices. In addition, the comic appearance of Titivillus on the scene —"I com wyth my leggys wnder me" (l. 454)—signals another sin in Mankind, namely, sloth. Titivillus was traditionally associated with sloth,[24] and he campaigns cleverly to induce it in Mankind. He makes him abandon his difficult planting by inserting a board in the ground to interfere with his shovel; and, when time comes for evensong, a whisper in the ear persuades Mankind to ignore it in favor of a nap. As Mankind lies down to sleep and starts snoring loudly, the laughter evoked in the audience is in recognition of his degeneration to the low level of partial existence induced in him by the vices. Substantial though the comic element is, therefore, it is integral and organic, a dimension in the portrayal of evil.

In *Nature* the evil chosen for homiletic mockery is personified in the vice called Sensuality, who offers humorous stories of tavern indulgence as well as satirical descriptions of abuses in monastic life. *Mundus et Infans* introduces the satirical vice Folye, who cheerfully tricks the gullible Infans into his service; characteristically, he lets the audience in on his wily plan:

> A ha! syrs, let the catte wynke!
> For all ye wote not what I thynke,
> I shall drawe hym suche a draught of drynke
> That Conscyence he shall awaye cast.
>
> (ll. 649–52)

He then satirizes the presence of his own brand of non-Being in London:

> By my faythe, in Englonde haue I dwelled yore,
> And all myne auncetters me before;
> But, syr, in London is my chefe dwellynge.
>
> (ll. 568–70)

Vice and victim now patronize the legal profession:

> For I am a seruant of the lawe;
> Couetous is myne owne felowe,
> We twayne plete for the kynge;
> And poore men that come from vplande,
> We wyll take theyr mater in hande,
> Be it ryght or be it wronge,
> Theyr thryfte with vs shall wende.
>
> (ll. 576–82)

And they live at ease among the clergy:

And with [the freres] I dwelled many yeres;
And they crowned Folye a kynge.

(ll. 601–2)

. . . .

In-to abbeys and in-to nonneryes also;
And alwaye Folye dothe felowes fynde.

(ll. 604–6)

The mockery of evil easily accommodates the mode of satire.

In the early English moralities, then, full-scope dramatizations of the life of everyman, the non-Being of evil is subjected to a consistent homiletic mockery. The lesson of the privative nature of evil is embodied in its worldly, fleshly, and diabolic manifestations, usually characterized on the physical level by rowdiness and bestiality, on the intellectual by deceit and equivocation.

Notes to Chapter 3

1. For discussion of the possible origins of the moral play, see the following: E. K. Chambers, *The Medieval Stage* (Oxford, 1903); Hardin Craig, "The Pater Noster Play," *Nation* 104 (1917): 563–64; J. M. Manly, "Literary Forms and the New Theory of the Origin of Species," *Modern Philology* 4 (1907) : 577–96; E. N. S. Thompson, *The English Moral Plays* (New Haven, Conn., 1910) .
2. The earliest extant play is the fragmentary *Pride of Life*; the earliest full-scope play is the *Castle of Perseverance.*
3. See Paul's Epistle to the Ephesians; Acts, *passim.*
4. Manly, "Literary Forms."
5. Gordon Leff, *Medieval Thought* (Harmondsworth, 1958) , p. 261.
6. Ockham, *Sentences* 1, dist. 2, q. 4, D, in *Philosophical Writings.*
7. See Gustave Reese, *Music in the Middle Ages* (New York, 1958) .

8. See Beryl Smalley, *The Study of the Bible in the Middle Ages* (Oxford, 1952); also Chambers, *Medieval Stage.*
9. Smalley, *Study of the Bible.*
10. For example, the *Blickling Homilies,* ed. R. Morris (London, 1880).
11. The most extensive extant drama is that of France. Approximately sixty-five French plays called moralities survive. For texts see the following editions: *Ancien Théâtre français,* ed. Viollet le Duc, 3 vols. (Paris, 1854); M. Edouard Fournier, *Le Théâtre français avant la renaissance,* 1450–1550 (Paris, 1874); Paul Lacroix, ed., *Recueil de farces, soties et moralités du quinzième siècle* (Paris, 1859); Robert Marichal, ed., *Le Théâtre en France au moyen age* (Paris, 1909); Johan Mortensen, ed., *Le Théâtre français au moyen age* (Paris, 1903); Gustave Cohen, *Mystères et moralités* (Paris, 1920); Gustave Cohen, *Recueil de farces inédites du XVe siècle* (Cambridge, Mass., 1949).
12. Examples of recent scholarship in cognizance of the morality influence include David Bevington, *From Mankind to Marlowe* (Cambridge, Mass., 1962); Hardin Craig, "Morality Plays and Elizabethan Drama," *Shakespeare Quarterly* 1 (1950): 64–72; Alan Dessen, "Volpone and the Late Morality Tradition," *Modern Language Quarterly* 25 (1964): 383–99; Alan Dessen, "The Alchemist: Jonson's 'Estates' Play," *Renaissance Drama* 7 (1964): 35–54; Bernard Spivack, "Falstaff and the Psychomachia," *Shakespeare Quarterly* 8 (1957): 449–59; Bernard Spivack, *Shakespeare and the Allegory of Evil* (New York, 1958).
13. *Pride of Life* in *Non-Cycle Plays and Fragments,* ed. Norman Davis (Oxford, 1970), pp. 90–105.
14. In *The Macro Plays,* ed. Mark Eccles (Oxford, 1969).
15. Ibid.
16. Ibid.
17. *Everyman,* reprinted by W. W. Greg from the edition of John Sket (Louvain, 1909). For discussion of the question of Dutch or English origin, see E. R. Tigg, "Is Elckerlyc Prior to Everyman?" *Journal of English and Germanic Philology* 38 (1939): 568–96 (argument for Dutch origin) and Henry de Vocht, "Everyman: A Comparative Study of Texts and Sources," *Materials for the Study of the Old English Drama* (Louvain, 1947) (argument for English origin).
18. Henry Medwall, *Nature,* ed. Alois Brandl, *Quellen.*
19. *Mundus et Infans,* ed. John M. Manly, *Specimens of the Pre-Shakespearean Drama,* 2 vols. (Boston, 1897), 1.
20. Most of the early and several of the late moralities have a "double-fall structure", i.e., Man, born innocent, falls initially into a life

of sin, interrupted by sporadic regrets and repentance; later he falls again, this time confirmed in sin and often brought to the point of suicidal despair.

21. Francesco Marias Guazzo, *Compendium Maleficorum*, ed. Rev. Montague Summers, trans. E. A. Ashwin (London, 1929).
22. Charles Gibbon, *Remedie of Reason* (London, 1589), G2v.
23. *The Macro Plays*, p. xvii.
24. Titivillus was traditionally associated with spiritual sloth. A legend was that he carried a huge bag containing the dropped final syllables of hymns and prayers recited and sung by slack Christians.

4

Homiletic Scorn

"Let them laffe in the end that the victorye doth winne" -- Politick Persuasion in *Patient and Meek Grissell,* 1. 957

1

THE moral mockery of evil continued throughout the sixteenth century, becoming ever more conventionalized in its dramatic forms. The humor that in the early, full-scope moralities heaped scorn on the heads of various personifications of evil, thereby demonstrating the privative nature of the world, the flesh, and the devil, evolved into a clear-cut and refined technique of homiletic comedy. And, throughout the long and successful history of the moral drama, this comic technique was to be reserved for the one function to which it had been originally assigned: the demonstration of evil. Not often does the humor deviate into either innocent merriment or gratuitous obscenity; the comic scenes usually serve a homiletic purpose. Apart from the scornful, often boisterous depiction of evil, the tone of these plays is always one of serious reverence. When the proportion of humor increases—as it does in the later moral drama—it is not so much a loss of didactic purpose altogether in favor of entertainment but rather a gradual disappearance of the virtues from the stage. What started as the dramatization of the conflict of good and evil tended to become more and more a demonstration of the seduction of evil, with a merely token display of virtuous resistance. In fact, when the English drama finally becomes secular and largely realistic, the one allegorical figure strong enough to survive in it—that last infirmity of a noble tradition—is the Vice.

The conventional comic techniques enveloping the figures of evil grow directly out of the homiletic purpose already described. Typically, since dramatic technique grows out of subject matter rather than the reverse, a shift in subject matter demands technical innovation. A mere urge to experiment does not produce a new subject. Consequently the allegorical techniques were gradually modified in keeping with the slowly shifting emphasis in subject. The aim of the comic methods was still to defeat the forces of evil by the exposure and mockery of their ultimate non-Being. The mockery, however, tended more and more to become a play-long demonstration of the ultimately futile but nonetheless lively, even amusing, operation of the Vice. Laughter at him merged with laughter with him as he came to share in the conclusions of his object-lesson, engaging in a great deal of self-mockery. Actually, the conventions of comedy attached to the portrayal of privative evil are clearly definable as they appear in the sixteenth-century moralities. These conventional techniques are exactly derived from and suited to those objects of mockery mentioned in the preceding chapter, namely, the world, the flesh, and the devil. There are three basic homiletic techniques for dealing with these three faces of evil, each with many variations.

First is the comic degradation of serious themes. This technique is an outgrowth of the mockery of the world; it is a means of revealing moral perspective through reversal of values. Evil as the absence of good, or as the falling short of complete Being, suggests a degraded form of the good that may thus be presented and subjected to a humorous but illuminating mockery. This technique of degradation is applied to such serious themes as death, virtue, scriptural history, the liturgy, and—in some ways its most subtle application—the very threat to salvation implicit in such debasement. Self-mockery of the vices combines with mockery of love, justice, loyalty, friendship, and similar ideas to present that grotesque reverse side of the coin of virtue which is inscribed with an evil grin.

Second, physical farce mocks the subject of the flesh. Farcical action, often uproarious and crude, exposes the nonspiritual, hence, nonessential nature of evil. Such low comic activity may take the form of violence or of bestiality. The vices engage repeatedly in physical quarrels and random beatings; they also participate in and endlessly discuss the processes of digestion, elimination, and sexuality. In order to project the lower nature of man convincingly, the vices must behave with concrete, "realistic" animal activity. Vice as an abstraction cannot personify violence or bestiality, hence the emphasis on low comedy.[1]

The third technique is verbal: the humorous manipulation and distortion of language comment on the fraudulent nature of evil just as degradation and farce comment on its worldly and bestial nature. Verbal humor directly mocks the devil, the father of lies. Even as evil is not what it seems to be, so its words do not mean what they seem to mean. The agents of evil are verbal jugglers and acrobats:

they make equivocal promises, swear mock oaths, and parody liturgical language and scriptural texts. Their words may be literally true but false to the spirit of their meaning, or they may be genuine only in sound, and completely false in meaning. The whole gamut of playful, equivocal, and misleading language is employed by the forces of evil, from the obvious pun to the Latinized sacrilege.

The hybrid play—partly allegorical and partly literal—that evolved from the moral drama, as well as the sixteenth-century moralities, illustrates these techniques of thematic degradation, equivocal language, and farcical action as they appertain consistently to the demonstration of evil.

2

One of the serious subjects held up to homiletic mockery throughout the transitional drama of the sixteenth century was that of death.[2] Since evil in its privative nature is dependent upon mortality for its functioning, it is very much the business of the vices to encourage the strictly mortal concerns of their victims. Unable to anticipate immortality themselves, the vices not only lure their victims to cling desperately to their fragile mortality, but they themselves, with equal desperation, resist threats to their own continued earthly survival. Thus we see many instances of the vices' refusal to die. In *Common Conditions*[3] the titular Vice finds himself threatened with hanging by the three tinkers named Shift, Drift, and Unthrift. Very much in the manner of imperturbable Barnardine in *Measure for Measure,* this Vice simply refuses to be hanged. He also asserts his devotion to this life in his advice to his mistress. When this unfortunate lady, saddened by the loss of her love, bemoans "I joy no longer life," he objects with the contrary opinion that "a mad fool he were, would desperately die, and never did offend." A descendant of the smirking, bony figure who appeared in the medieval Dance of Death scenes,[4] the sixteenth-century Vice continues to divert humanity from its proper concern with salvation, stressing instead the mortal satisfaction of earthly survival.

Similarly, in *Virtuous and Godly Susanna*,[5] the Vice called Ill Report is threatened with hanging, after his trickery and sophistry are duly exposed by the perceptive True Report. But even as the jailer casts his rope about the neck of the reluctant Vice, Ill Report remains quick-witted and clever, immediately protesting "why, Knave, wilt thou choke me?" and then requesting a stay in order that he may say his Pater Noster first. When the stay is granted, he retorts:

Now by my Fathers soule thou art an honest man,
And since thou doest so gently that tyme to me giue,
I will not say my Pater noster, whyle I haue a day to liue,
And if you shall at tyme heare that I so do,
Then hang me hardely and draw me to.

(ll. 1373–77)

Finding himself in an analogous position is the Vice Iniquity in the play of *Nice Wanton*.[6] When he is arrested along with Ishmael, the youth whom he has corrupted into leading a debauched and wicked life, he tries to elude all punishment. In spite of his protests, the judge orders him hanged. But Iniquity fights off the halter, unscrupulously volunteers Ishmael's neck for sacrifice instead of his, and finally feigns righteous indignation, maintaining equivocally "if thou shouldest hange me, I were a-curst." (l. 419) Led off to execution together with his victim, he first announces hopefully that he has influential friends and then offers instead to become a servant (and master, he slyly adds) of anyone in the audience who will save him.

In *Like Will to Like*,[7] the Vice called Nichol Newfangle assumes the role of judge of his fellow roisterers early in the play only later on to fall victim to genuine judgment himself. Near the end of the play, Nichol appears ominously with two halters, but he abandons them in favor of singing songs and hawking wares to the audience. When the Judge, this time named Severity, enters the scene, he permits Nichol to help him place the halters about the necks of the evildoers, who are by this time quite repentant of their bad deeds. The ironic humor of the scene occurs in the sudden turnabout that happens at this point. Just as the confident Nichol and the grim Hankin Hangman are about to share between them the coats of the condemned men, Lucifer appears on the scene to seize the indignant Vice and carry him off to hell.

In the late morality called *The Contention between Liberality and Prodigality*,[8] the titular figure of Prodigality clings tenaciously to life and resists death with fierce humor. In this play, which is reminiscent of Dante's treatment of the hoarders and spendthrifts in the Inferno, several conventional medieval themes persist. The figure of Prodigality comes near death twice. In one scene, as he tries to scale the wall of Fortune's palace, the figure of Fortune appears to place a halter around the neck of the intruder. When Prodigality then slips and almost chokes, he breaks into abusive anger: "O thou vile, ill-fauoured, crow-troden, pyepecked Ront!/ Thou abominable, blinde, foule filth. . . ." Escaping fatality this time, he is later sentenced to death but spared when he repents. (ll. 908–9).

In all of these plays, the death of the hero—whether threatened or actual—is treated with utmost seriousness, whereas the death of the vice or villain becomes a subject for the humor of mockery.

Similarly, virtue becomes a double theme, treated with complementary mockery and reverence throughout the transitional drama. The vices, by definition images of perversion and deprivation, mock the good through effective and ingenious disguises in virtue's garb. Evil is not what it seems to be: under a virtuous exterior may lurk a dangerous vice.

In the *Life and Repentance of Mary Magdalene*,[9] the vices introduce themselves honestly to the audience but assume fitting disguises for presentation to their intended victim. Infidelity reveals his identity candidly:

> Infidelitie is my name, you know in dede,
> Properly I am called the Serpent's sede.
> Loke, in whose heart my Father Sathan doth me sow,
> There must all iniquities and vice nedes growe.
>
> (ll. 1235–38)

And Pride boasts to the audience that he is all the vices in one:

> For I my selfe not onely conteyne you three,
> But all vices in you, and that in every degree.
>
> (ll. 339–40)

But Pride, the root evil that fosters all of the other deadly sins, assumes a disguise for the purpose of deceiving Mary Magdalene. Infidelity becomes Prudence; Pride, Nobility and Honor; Concupiscence, Pleasure; and Cupiditie, Utility.

During this transitional period of the drama, political subjects were introduced into moralities. One of the greatest political moralities, John Skelton's *Magnificence*,[10] carries on the traditional stage treatment of evil. Here the political vices mockingly degrade their virtuous counterparts through disguise: Cloaked Collusion becomes sober Sadness; Counterfeit Countenance becomes Good Demeanance. Cloaked Collusion even amplifies the principle of disguise, adding to it humorous equivocation:

> Double Delynge and I be all one;
> Craftynge and haftynge contryued is by me;

I can dyssemble, I can bothe laughe and grone;
Playne Delynge and I can neuer agre;
But Dyuysyon, Dyssencyon, Dyrysyon,—these thre,
And I, am counterfet of one mynde and thought,
By the menys of Myschyef to bryng all thynges to nought.

(ll. 696–702)

In the political morality of *Respublica,*[11] the villainous figure of Avarice easily assumes the convincing disguise of Policy, and his companion in crime, Adulation, deftly passes himself off as Honesty. Further humor ensues, moreover, when clever Avarice tries to teach his slow-witted companion "Honesty" his new name:

Avarice: "Polycye, I saide, Policye, Knave, Polycye."
Nowe saye as I sayd.
Adulation: "Policie, Knave, Policie!"

(ll. 403–4)

The reluctant pupil causes further comic trouble by acting in accordance with the spirit of the new name, frankly revealing the fraudulent plot to deluded Lady Respublica:

Madame, the cause of all this was Avarice;
He forged us new names, and dyd us all entice.

Several other plays incorporate the renaming of vices as a humorous device for mocking their hypocritical pose as virtues. In *New Custom*[12] Perverse and Ignorance come to be called Sound Doctrine and Simplicity; in the fragmentary morality called *Albion Knight,*[13] Injury wins the friendship of Albion by professing to be Manhood; and in the moralized romance of *Sir Clyomon and Sir Clamydes,*[14] the Vice named Subtle Shift masquerades before his master as Knowledge. Not always do the vices rename themselves; sometimes the central Vice assumes the prerogative of renaming his subordinates. In *Enough Is As Good As A Feast,*[15] Covetous renames his cohorts as follows: Inconsideration is called Reason; Temerity is called Agility; and Precipitation is called Ready Wit. Their duties spring logically from their names: Temerity is "to do all things without delay," Precipitation is "to see and do all without forecast," and Inconsideration is "to consider neither the time, the person, nor the place."

Another pervasive example of mockery is one much less readily recognized by the modern reader, a more hedonistic individual, perhaps, than his medieval ancestors. Throughout the moral drama there is repeated emphasis on the dangers of what *seems* to be innocent merriment. Even the delights of music are suspect in these homiletic pieces, and often the humor of what appears to be merely congenial party spirit is itself a condemnation of a serious threat to salvation. In *The Marriage Between Wit and Wisdom,*[16] the battery of charming vices who mislead young Wit includes Idleness posing as Honest Recreation, and Wantonness pretending to be Modest Mirth.[17] The seductive formula inherent in such amusements is explained by two vices in *The Tide Tarrieth No Man.*[18] They explicate their roles in a song:

> Though wastfulnesse and wantonnesse,
> Some men haue us two named,
> Yet pleasauntnesse and plyauntnesse,
> Our names we haue now framed.
>
> (ll. 1337–40)

It is a significant and often misunderstood fact that the use of music in the moral drama is almost always associated with the worldly distractions of evil. Secular singing and dancing are more likely to be tools of the devil than harmless recreation.

Still another aspect of comic degradation is the deliberat
parody of a specific serious action through episodes analo
gous either to the play or to familiar scriptural material
In the many examples of the latter, a parodic version o
either words or incidents taken from the Scriptures serve
to comment comically on evil. Such examples are of cours
in the tradition of the Second Shepherd's Play of th
Towneley cycle, with its ingenious parody of the nativity.[1
In *Virtuous and Godly Susanna*,[20] when the innocent heroin
faints in court from the shock of false accusations brough
against her, the Vice attempts to revive her with mustar
and vinegar, evoking the familiar scene of Calvary. A parodi
version of language occurs in *Like Will to Like*, where th
Vice Nichol Newfangle applies to Lucifer a phrase tradi
tionally applied to God: "was, is, and ever shall be."

The same play will also serve to illustrate the use o
contrapuntal parody. Early in the action, Nichol Newfangl
acts as judge, deciding among his tavern companions wh
is to act as knave of clubs at Christmas time. The procedur
of formal trial and judgment recurs later in the play, whe
the proper judge, named Severity, inflicts heavy sentence
on those same roistering knaves for their bad behavior
Another such instance occurs in *Three Laws*,[20] where th
Vice Infidelitas parodies the theme of Moses' receiving th
divine tablets. Much parody that is at once scriptural an
contrapuntal characterizes this theological morality devote
to proving the identity of natural law, the law of Moses, an
Christian law.

The attributes of the vices are also mocked in the didacti
determination to display their ultimate powerlessness. T
those innocents who do not penetrate the deceptive exterio
of vice to discover its underlying ineffectuality and insubstantiality, the weapons of evil look threatening indeed.
Consequently the vices are often portrayed comically as
armed with a medley of ineffective or absurd weapons. Ex-

amples of the amusing revelation of the impotence of evil hrough exposure of harmless weapons appear in many plays. n *Wit and Science,*[21] the recalcitrant hero, Wit, almost orfeits his opportunity for a good match with Reason's laughter, Science, because he falls prey to Tediousness, a nonster (evil, although not specifically a vice) who enters he play wearing a visor and singing a vain threat:

> Where art thow, Wyt?
> Thow art but deade!
> Of goth thy hed
> A' the fyrst blow!
> Ho, ho! ho, ho!
>
> (ll. 188–92)

The vanity of the threat is made clear when Wit, momen-arily struck down by the monster, is quickly revived by he ministrations of Honest Recreation, Comfort, Quickness, and Strength.

In *Albion Knight,* the vice who threatens with grotesquely useless weapons is Division, described scornfully as:

> A lustye Captayne,
> A Boore with a tuske,
> A sturdie Luske.
>
> (ll. 170–72)

In both of Richard Wilson's late allegorical plays, *The Three Ladies of London* and *The Three Lords and Three Ladies of London,*[22] evil figures bear mock weapons. In the irst play, Fraud appears in a sword and buckler, which seem real until he attacks Simplicity, when their ineffective-ness is made manifest. It is in the second play, however, that an almost archetypal instance of the futility of evil is en-acted. In this subsequent encounter between Simplicity and

Fraud, the good man is able by virtue of his honesty to burn Fraud into nothingness. Few episodes illustrate more incisively the empty aspirations of evil and its ultimate destruction.

Finally, the embodiments of evil in the moral drama degrade themselves through their own absurd laughter. Mocking their own pretentious existence, relishing their virtuosity in seduction, chuckling over their fiendish plots, the vices themselves are the comical center of the morality tradition. Examples of the laughter characteristic of these demonic diverters are legion. A few must suffice here. In *The Conflict of Conscience,*[23] laughter at once grim and grotesque, ominous and hilarious, marks the victory of Hypocrisy over Philologus. The former gloats over his fallen victim, maintaining cheerfully, "Such chopping chears, as we haue made, the like hath not bin seene" (l. 1919). His triumphant outburst fulfills the optimistic anticipation expressed earlier in the play, when he chuckled, "ha, ha, ha, mary now the Game beginne" (l. 804). Similarly, in *Enough Is As Good As A Feast,* the Vice also appears over the body of his expiring victim, gloating in gleeful satisfaction over his accomplishment. The physician who attends the victim, named Worldly Man, objects to Covetous's jesting at such a serious moment. But Covetous will not be suppressed and enjoys the entire scene, particularly the stupid inefficiency of Ignorance in attempting to take down his master's will by dictation. The stupidity is transmuted into profanity when the sacred name is omitted: "in the name, in, in, in the name, what more?" And when Satan enters the death room to claim one more lost soul for his kingdom, Covetous is buoyed even further in spirit by final proof of his success, as the devil chants triumphantly, "oh, oh, oh, oh, all is mine."

Other vices, energetically asserting their cheer in the pursuit of the wholesale corruption of mankind, appear in *Trial* of *Treasure*[24] and *King Darius*.[25] Inclination, in the former play, proclaims delightedly his intervention in the struggle of Just and Lust: "Better sport in my life I never saw." Momentarily bridled by Just, he is subsequently set free by Lust and returns, laughing merrily at his fortune: "Am I not in blessed case, Treasure and Pleasure to possess?" And Iniquity, the frisky vice in the half-biblical play of *King Darius*, disdains the pleas of Equity, scoffing at them with uncontrollable laughter: "He, ha, ha, ha, I muste nedes laugh;/ Get thee away, knaue, and go draw the ploughe" (ll. 405–6). Commenting for all vices, he remarks on his own cheerful and irrepressible energy: "If I do not bestyre my selfe, I shall decaye" (l. 408).

The vices continued throughout the transitional and hybridized moral drama to demonstrate the comedy of evil through the traditional technique of comic degradation of serious themes. At the same time they were supported by a verbal convention that becomes the next consideration.

3

Just as evil is not what it seems to be, its words do not mean what they seem to say. The language of evil is by definition equivocal, and the vices of the moralities indulge in continual comic distortion and manipulation of language. The danger in their verbal witchery is that they do not merely tell lies, but they tell lies that sound like the truth. They debase language not through falsehood but through fraudulence. The voices of evil make promises that are not invalid but misleading; they take oaths that are not wrong but wanton; they echo the sacred liturgy, not mistakenly but sacrilegiously. The tragic lesson learned by Macbeth, that the alluring voices of evil "palter with us in a double sense," and "keep the word of promise to our ear, and break it to our hope" (5. 8), is learned by a century of morality protagonists who precede him.

An example of the promises of evil that have a litera validity but an ultimate deception occurs in *Like Will t Like*. Nichol Newfangle offers to his victims, two dedicate thieves named Cuthbert Cutpurse and Pierce Pickpurse, gift of land:

> I promised of late a piece of land,
> Which by & by shall fall into your hand.
>
> (ll. 1099–1100

But they later learn exactly what Macbeth learns about th promises that are kept to the ear but broken to the hope To their horror and undoing, the "land" is in reality th gallows spot, which will indeed be their inheritance Newfangle then gloats over his successful joke, confiding t the audience:

> Ah, my masters, how like you this play?
> You shall take possession of your land today!
> I will help to bridle the two-legged mare,
> And both you for to ride need not to spare.
>
> (ll. 1122–25

Later he cynically casts lots with Hankin Hangman for th coats of the convicted and condemned thieves. The sam play also includes an example of the mock oath, that favorit comic device by which a serious oath is repeated by an evi character using words that sound almost identical but in actuality mean something entirely different. When Lucife would have Nichol swear to "exalt thee above the clouds,' sly Nichol replies with solemn-sounding wit, "to salt thee and hang thee in shrouds."

Instances of comic equivocation occur in almost every

ıorality, but only a few will be cited here to represent this remendously popular way of revealing the deceitful nature f evil. First, in the biblical play of *Virtuous and Godly usanna,* Satan appears only briefly, and fails to dominate his mpudent agent, Ill Report. In an attempt to cajole this ice who performs his evil seduction for him, he gives a ıock blessing, offering his aide "all that God gave to Cain nd Jonah and Nineveh." Surely such humorous equivocaion "lies like truth." Similarly, in *The Tide Tarrieth No Ian* the versatile Vice Courage is full of such equivocation. His activity as Vice is to "incourage" several susceptible ndividuals into un-Christian and worldly conduct:

> Now may you see how Corage can worke,
> And how he can encorage both to good and bad:
> The Marchaunt is incouraged, in greedinesse to lurke
> And the Courtyer to win worship, by Corage is glad.
> The one is good, no man will denay,
> I meane corage to win worship and fame:
> So that the other is ill, all men will say,
> That is corage to greedinesse, which getteth ill name.
> Thus may you see Corage contagious,
> And eake contrarious, both in me do rest.
>
> (ll. 698–707)

And it is his "encouragement" of greed that occupies the entral action of the play. When the figure of Greediness uccumbs, a lonely miser in his hour of death, and is carried on the tide-boat to hell quite unmourned by anyone, Courage comes in as the sole mourner, weeping and conessing candidly, "I weep as much as any one!"

Similarly, in *Godly Queen Hester*[26] the Vice Hardy Dardy peaks with an amusingly naive literalness. When he requests he traditional fool's prerogative to speak freely, he takes dvantage of the opportunity to warn Haman of the genuine danger to the future of that malicious chancellor who plans to massacre the Jews, people of the godly queen. He comments brightly on his dire prediction:

> Men say in dede, ye shall lose your head,
> And that woulde make you stumble.
>
> (ll. 799–800)

Another category of verbal humor is the sacrilegious parody of liturgy. A play that exemplifies this technique is *Impatient Poverty*,[27] where the character of Misrule appears on the scene, speaking mock French while inciting to irreligious revelry:

> Venir aueuque vous gentyl compaygnon
> Faictes bone chere pour lamour de sainct Iohn
> Mon coeur iocunde is sette on a mery pynne
> By my trouth I am disposed to reuelynge.
>
> (ll. 611–14)

Misrule is a medieval inheritance: the mock figure dates back to medieval rituals of misrule and disorder.[28] In a somewhat similar vein, liturgical language is parodied extensively in John Bale's late morality, *King Johan*.[29] The focus in evil is on the vice Dissimulation, who appoints to each group of characters specific roles in performance of the sacred mass:

> To wynne the peple, I appoynt yche man his place:
> Sum to syng Latyn, and sum to ducke at grace;
> Sum to go mummyng, and sum to beare the crosse;
> Sum to stowpe downeward as the[r] heades ware stopt with mosse;
> Sum rede the epystle and gospell at hygh masse;
> Sum syng at the lectorne with long eares lyke an asse.
>
> (ll. 697–702)

In this Protestant morality concerning the conflict of church and state, the object of the parody is Catholic ritual. Later in the play, the vice Sedition imitates the ritual performed by the priest, whom he considers a very jolly fellow, with "pipys and belles with kyre, kyrey, lyrye."

Ignorance of Scripture and of other holy matters was a serious vice to the Christian mind of the time. Consequently, such ignorance also comes in for its share of mockery as a privative evil. Perhaps the most amusing personification of ignorance is the figure who appears in *Enough Is As Good As A Feast*. Characteristically, Ignorance ignores the earnest warnings of the Prophet and threats of the impending Plague, persisting in the blindness of his nature. He maintains that he is quite able to recite Scripture in Latin, but when he insists upon demonstrating that dubious ability, the result is a linguistic hodgepodge:

> Magistorum clericium inkepe miorum
> Totus perus altus, yongus at oldus
> Multus knavoribus et quoque fasorum
> Pickpursus omnius argentus shavus et polus.
>
> (ll. 1265–68)

Parody is not only a matter of language for these dramatic personifications of evil but also a matter of action. The double-plot structure, which occurs early in the hybrid moralities, becomes an opportunity for parodic exploitation of serious, sometimes scriptural, episodes. In the *Life and Repentance of Mary Magdalene,* for instance, the main plot, in which the Vice Malicious Judgment collects false testimony against Christ, is paralleled and parodied by the subplot, in which the comic vices of Pride of Lyfe, Cupiditie, and Carnall Concupiscence seduce and malign Mary Magdalene. The two plots are joined through the Vice Infidelity, who moves from one to the other, remaining throughout

the jolly companion, at one point taking part in a quartet of vices, accompanied by Mary Magdalene on the virginal:

> He, dery, dery, with a lusty dery,
> Hoigh, mistresse Mary, I pray you be mery.
>
> (ll. 783–84)

Through comic manipulation of language, involving parody, equivocation, misinterpretation, and misapplication, the vices augment their comic role throughout the transitional, often hybridized plays. The language of evil is as misleading as its appearance and its actions; both are fraudulent, but humor is released in the recognition of the fraudulent exterior.

4

The lavish intrusion of farce into the serious dramatization of man's spiritual life has provoked condemnation of the literary merit of the moralities. Rowdy, obscene, boisterous farce, however, is one of the central techniques of dramatizing the comedy of evil. The word *farce* originally meant "stuffing"[30] and was applied to interpolations in the liturgy. By analogy the word came to refer not only to the dramatic episodes so interpolated but also to the specifically comic incidents that were to become a conventional part of the mystery cycles. Since this comic byplay was largely based on action and situation as well as on language, the word *farce* became associated with broad physical humor, and because this slapstick comedy continued to be "stuffed" into the moralities, it continued to demonstrate one particular facet of the privative nature of evil.

The farcical elements in the hybrid plays as well as in the moralities were concerned with representing the lower nature of man, the fallen, mortal flesh. For the most part

the farce consists of violence, bestiality, and obscenity. Both vices and their human victims are continually engaged, on the one hand, in brawling and beatings, and on the other, in frankly obscene manifestations of and references to the sexual and cloacal aspects of existence. In the same tradition as Dante's demons, cited earlier in connection with their farcical activity described in the twenty-first and twenty-second cantos of the *Inferno,* the vices carried on decades of violent and obscene activity, shocking the decorous virtues while they amused—and ostensibly enlightened—the audience.

On occasion the Vice fights with either his supposed master, the devil, or with his intended victim, a human. In *All for Money,*[31] the allied figures of Sin and Satan quarrel over superiority. Satan, who appears "as deformedly dressed as can be," is challenged in his arrogant merriment ("ohe, ohe, I was never so merie") by Sin, who scornfully reminds him that the devil—whom he insultingly calls "snottienose" —is quite helpless without the aid of sin. After a brief but lusty dispute, Sin emerges triumphant, and Satan is left roaring with pain and humiliation.

The prodigal son play of *Nice Wanton* will serve as an example of the Vice's physical quarrel with his victim. In this play the misguided heroine, Delilah, fights vigorously with the Vice Iniquity over their combined winnings from gambling. Iniquity subdues her with a hearty box on the ears, doubtless to the merriment of the audience. Frequently such quarrels are quite unmotivated, and they occur as inevitable manifestations of the disorderly nature of evil. To cite one example out of many, in *The Cruel Debtor*[32] Rigor and Simulation obviously fight for absolutely no other reason than their essential and inescapable propensity to do so. The divisive and destructive nature of evil must show itself in this gratuitous pugnacity. "I can chide, fight, and be mery," boasts the Vice in *Hickscorner.*

But evil is bestial as well as violent. The humor of obscenity has a definite homiletic place in the comedy of evil alongside the humor of physical altercation. Again, from the many examples available, a few will serve to illustrate the popularity of the tradition. In *Enough Is As Good As A Feast,* when the unfortunate Worldly Man falls ill, he is attended by the Vice Covetous. After praying mockingly to St. Uncumber, the Vice suggests an obscene physical examination to the doctor. Since the worldliness of the protagonist has led him to overemphasize the all-too-mortal flesh, this death ironically conjoins the themes of mortality and sensuality with evil. In *All For Money,* the theme of physical excess is dominant. Logically, the entire sequence of the protagonist's submission to vice is demonstrated through the bestial process of regurgitation. The series of digestive upsets begins when Money becomes "sick." From a trap door conveniently provided for such dramatic exigencies, "comes up" the character of Pleasure, who in turn becomes sick, yielding up Prest-for-Pleasure. The chain continues, with Sin being "thrown up," followed ultimately by Damnation. Sin explains the moral lesson of these upheavals:

Do you not see how all is for money, masters?
His money brings him to pleasure, and pleasures send him to me,
And I send him to Damnation, and he sends him to hell quickly.

(ll. 1313, 1317–18)

The device is dramaturgically effective as well as funny, and it is tempting to speculate whether Ben Jonson found in it an inspiration for his brilliantly satirical scene based on the same device in *The Poetaster.*

5

A look at three late transitional plays—blatant specimens

of what Sidney called "mongrel" drama—will carry this discussion of the comedy of evil in morality and hybrid drama up to the threshhold of the Elizabethan drama proper. Two particular facts invite attention in these plays from the generation preceding Marlowe. One is that although the abstractions of virtue diminish, the abstraction of the Vice is not merely retained but becomes the dominating figure in the manipulation of dramatic action. His structural function becomes more sophisticated and complex. No longer does he merely tempt and goad a susceptible human victim, but he purveys the theme of his particular nature on several separate levels of action. He begins to operate in thematic counterpoint, as a kind of germ carrier infecting one or more sets of characters besides the hero, always with varying degrees of humor. In a primarily tragic context his infections provide comic counterpoint; and in a primarily comic context, by way of dramatic contrast, he evokes dark, satiric laughter rather than confident, light-hearted merriment. The second fact is that the comedy of evil is by no means limited to the Vice. The dramaturgic devices associated traditionally with the comedy of evil, however, function to identify literal characters as evil. Even where the language does not make it explicit, familiar devices such as the tears and laughter, the violence and bawdry, the equivocation and other verbal trickery constitute a symbolic mode of communicating the presence of evil.

The popular play of *Cambises,*[33] which the Elizabethans fondly recalled for its sensationalism and bombastic language, injects into the historical episodes involving a cruel Persian king the lively figure of Ambidexter, "one that with both hands finely can play." This double-dealing Vice retains the conventional techniques of his ancestors. He mocks the subject of war and at the same time betrays his own impotence when he appears armed with kitchen utensils:

Enter the Vice, with an old capcase on his head, an olde

paile about his hips for harnes, a scummer and a potlid by his side, and a rake on his shoulder. (scene 2)

His boasting words are hollow:

> Stand away, stand away, for the passion of God!
> Harnassed I am, prepared to the field!
>
> (scene 2, 1–2)

When the ruffianly soldiers Huf, Ruf, and Snuf attack him and are joined by the spirited meretrix "with a staffe on her shoulder," he runs away with a Falstaffian rationalization on his lips: "It is wisdom (quoth I) by the mass, to save me!" (ll. 1170). Throughout the play he betrays amusingly his unsubstantiality, and at the conclusion, when the king by bizarre, ironic justice is stabbed with his own sword, Ambidexter flees to avoid the charge of murder. He illustrates throughout the play the humor of obscenity, equivocation, and degradation.

Similarly, the popular legend dramatized as *Patient Grissell*[34] adopts the Vice, this time called Politick Persuasion, to motivate the action:

> Nowe Pollitické Perswasion, nowe or els neuer,
> Phie, for chaffing I can skant keepe my teeth to gether,
> I tell you I haue found out such an inuension,
> As among the common sort, shall kindle discencion.
>
> (ll. 889–92)

He proceeds to urge Janice to test the angelic patience of Grissell through those drastic torments which the legend has made familiar. When the Marquis begins to repent of his severity, Politick Persuasion eggs him on:

> Be frollicke and ioyfull set sorowes aparte,

Are you not ashamed to blubber and weepe,
It is time now to playe the man, and not a symple sheepe,
Procead forward faint not, your purpose prosequte,
Be not reputed a coward, the fackt excequte.

(ll. 1581–85)

In line with the conventional representations of comic evil, he indulges in mock oaths and grotesque self-eulogy. Iago-like, he asserts his honesty: "I am an honist man,/ Some bodye can tell that I use not to lie," (ll. 379–80) and denies flattering: "I speak plainlye I can not flatter" (l. 419). And he parodies a blessing, with obscene degradation echoing the words:

Nowe God of his grace, in your choyce sende you good lucke,
And graunt that your loue maye laste for euer

(ll. 206–7)

becomes:

I beseech God send you with her, as manye hornes as a Bucke,
That your tounge, her nose, & my tayle: may be ioyned togither.

(ll. 208–9)

The retention of the Vice, striking as it is in these otherwise literal dramas, is not so significant, however, as the expansion of the role through contrapuntal action. Three plays from the 1560s and 1570s illustrate this new structural function of the vestigial Vice, a function that was to remain active in the Elizabethan theater long after the Vice's descendants had lost the generic name in favor of specific and literal nomenclature. Starting modestly with variations on a theme, the Vice maneuvers into other groups of characters beyond his concentrated attack on one particular victim; eventually his activities grow into a whole contrapuntal plot, refocusing and contrasting the main plot. But first let us examine the beginning of this structural role on the pre-Marlovian stage.

In 1563 appeared the tragedy of *Apius and Virginia*,[35] based on the Latin story of the virtuous girl who preferred death to dishonor. The simple narrative is complicated through the addition of morality elements. To the principals of the stark plot—the father, his heroically chaste daughter, and the lustful judge whose unbridled desire brings about the tragedy—are added three new sets of characters: several abstractions, all pale didactic figures named Rumor, Comfort, Conscience, Justice, Reward, Doctrine, and Memory; the servants, Subservus, Mansipula, and Mansipulas; and the irrepressible figure of the Vice, Haphazard. It becomes clear from the opening scene that the conflict between good and evil has a different focus from that of the original story. Virginia and her parents chant in smug harmony: "trustiest treasure . . . Is man, wife, and children in one to agree." The admirable filial solidarity is seemingly duplicated on a lower level, among the domestic staff, where Mansipula and Mansipulas, a man-and-wife team, in turn work together agreeably with Subservus. But the Vice Haphazard appears on the happy scene, announcing his own nature: a devotee of chance, he scorns the ethic of human concord. His actions are presented contrapuntally around this central theme of family harmony. Before he destroys the Christian household of Virginius by bringing about the death of the maiden daughter at the hands of her father, he creates comic strife in the servants' domicile. He intervenes among the trio, creating discord first between husband and wife, then between them and Subservus. Soon all three forget their former harmonious relationship and indulge in humorous but violent contention, name-calling, and fighting. It is only after the theme of family unity has been comically degraded in this subplot that we see the disastrous insinuations of the "hap as hap can" figure pervert the honest judge into the reckless adventurer who resolves flippantly to follow the Vice's amoral code—"I will, hap woe or wealth." Further enforcing the homiletic theme, already introduced in the subplot, the judge then ignores the figures of Conscience and Justice, armed respectively with lamp and sword, who try to dissuade him from his dishonorable plan. It is too late, for Apius is seduced, and his own dialogue becomes essentially indistinguishable from that of the Vice:

Apius: Well, hap as can hap, hap or no,
In hazard it is, but let that goe.

(ll. 856–57)

Haphazard: Hope so, and hap so, in hazard of thret'ninge
The worst that can hap, lo, in end is but beating.

(ll. 285–86)

Haphazard thus functions homiletically on two levels, illustrating the theme of family discord on both, with an ironic role on the tragic level and a more farcical role devoted to degrading the serious theme on the subplot level.

Horestes,[36] another tragedy on a classical theme, appeared in 1567. It also ranges far in tone from the stark original, with added dimensions in all directions to convert the narrative into a moral exemplum. The theme of revenge is personified in the person of the Vice. In keeping with his ancestral habit, however, Revenge changes his name frequently. He manages to insinuate himself into Horestes' confidence by presenting himself as Courage. But throughout the play, while the dire act of revenge is taking shape, the Vice also functions with equal zest and relentless humor on an entirely different level of action. Still illustrating the evils of revenge, he operates on the rustics Hodge and Rusticus, whom he incites to quarreling by incongruously introducing himself as Patience. The clowns, with their English rural dialect, at least mention King Aegisthus, lest their presence in ancient Greece seem wholly whimsical. When the Vice leaves, they make up their silly quarrel and retire to drink ale. Later in the action, Revenge engages in a similar routine with two soldiers, Haltersticke and Hempstring. Once more the two forget their desire for revenge promptly after the departure of the Vice. Both minor episodes are contrapuntal to the main theme: the pending tragic revenge is mocked by these cases of foolishly motivated and readily abandoned revenge.

Damon and Pithias,[37] staged in 1571, provides one more example of a classical story remade for the English stage. Although the play does not have the Vice, it does have the comedy of evil. The central plot, involving devoted friendship, is supported by two analogous lines of action. One is a mocking parallel to the Damon-Pithias fidelity and heroism. Aristippus, a "pleasant gentleman" of the court who is meretricious in his courtly ambition, vows eternal friendship with Cariophus the Parasite, who never honors any vow. The hypocritical conversation of the two provides a running commentary mocking the friendship theme. The other line of action occurs on a still lower level, where the respective servants of Aristippus and Cariophus engage in their own uncouth brand of insincere friendship. They join in amity only long enough to "shave" Grim the collier, a dupe to their dishonesty.

Whether or not in the person of the Vice, the comic exposure of evil continues, then, on the Elizabethan stage at the very threshhold of its golden age.

Notes to Chapter 4

1. Under the aegis of the naturalistic movement, violence and bestiality have become identified with "realistic" character portrayal. In retrospect, the low comedy of the vices becomes in turn "realism."
2. See the discusssion of the Dance of Death theme in chap. 2.
3. *Common Conditions* (1576), ed. C. F. Tucker-Brooke, in *Elizabethan Club Reprints* (New Haven, Conn., 1915).
4. See n. 2.
5. Thomas Garter, *Virtuous and Godly Susanna* (1578–79), ed B. I. Evans and W. W. Greg (Malone Society Reprint, Oxford, 1937).
6. *Nice Wanton* (1547–53), in *Specimens of the Pre-Shakespearian Drama,* ed. John M. Manly (Boston, 1897), 1.
7. Ulpian Fulwell, *Like Will to Like* (1562–68), in *A Select Collection of Old English Plays,* ed. Robert Dodsley, 4th ed. rev. by W. C. Hazlitt (London, 1874–76), 3.
8. *The Contention Between Liberality and Prodigality* (1567–68), ed. W. W. Greg. Malone Society Reprint, Oxford, 1913.
9. Lewis Wager, *Life and Repentance of Mary Magdalene* (ca. 1550), ed. F. I. Carpenter (Chicago, 1902).
10. John Skelton, *Magnificence* (1513–16), ed. Robert L. Ramsey (Oxford, 1908).
11. *Respublica* (1553), ed. L. A. Magnus (Oxford, 1905).
12. *New Custom* (1559–73), in Dodsley, ed., *A Select Collection,* vol. 3.
13. *Albion Knight* (1537–65), ed. W. W. Greg, Malone Society Collections, 1 and 3 (1909).
14. *Clyomon and Clamydes* (1570–83), ed W. W. Greg, Malone Society Reprint, (Oxford, 1913).
15. W. Wager, *Enough Is As Good As A Feast,* ed. Mark Benbow (Lincoln, Neb., 1967).
16. *Marriage between Wit and Wisdom* (Francis Merbury?), ed. J. O. Halliwell, Shakespeare Society, vol. 31 (London, 1846).
17. The scene recalls the mirthful figure of Acrasia in bk. 2 of *The Faerie Queene.*
18. George Wapull, *The Tide Tarrieth No Man* (1576), ed. E. Ruhl, *Jahrbuch* 43 (1907).
19. See chap. 1, passim.
20. John Bale, *Three Laws* (1530–36), ed. A. Schroeer, in *Anglia,* vol. 5 (1882).
21. John Redford, *Wit and Science* (1536–46), in *Specimens of the Pre-Shakespearian Drama,* ed. Manly, vol. 1.

22. Robert Wilson, *Three Ladies of London* and *Three Lords and Three Ladies of London* (1581; 1589), in *A Select Collection of Old English Plays,* ed. Dodsley, vol. 6.
23. Nathaniel Woodes, *Conflict of Conscience* (1575–81), ed. Herbert Davis and F. P. Wilson (Oxford, 1952).
24. *Trial of Treasure* (1567), ed. J. O. Halliwell, Percy Society, vol. 28 (London, 1850).
25. *King Darius* (1559–65), in *Quellen des weltlichen Dramas in England,* ed. Alois Brandl (Strasbourg, 1898).
26. *Godly Queen Hester* (1525–29), in *Materialien zur Kunde des alteren Englischen Dramas,* ed. W. Bang, vol. 5 (Louvain, 1904).
27. *Impatient Poverty* (1547–58), in *Materialien,* vol. 33 (1911).
28. See chap. 2, passim.
29. John Bale, *King Johan* (1530–36), in *Specimens,* Manly, vol. 1.
30. Middle English *fars,* stuffing; Middle French, *farce;* late Latin, *farsa.*
31. Thomas Lupton, *All for Money* (1559–77), in *English Morality Plays and Moral Interludes,* ed. Edgar T. Schell and J. D. Shuchter (New York, 1969).
32. *Cruel Debtor,* ed. W. W. Greg, Malone Society Collections (Oxford, 1911 and 1923).
33. Thomas Preston, *Cambises* (1558–69), in *Specimens,* ed. Manly, vol. 2.
34. John Phillip, *Patient and Meek Grissell,* ed. W. W. Greg, Malone Society Reprint (Oxford, 1909).
35. *Apius and Virginia,* ed. R. B. McKerrow, Malone Society Reprint (Oxford, 1911).
36. John Pickering, *Horestes,* in *Quellen,* ed. Brandl, Malone Society Reprint (Oxford, 1962).
37. R. Edward, *Damon and Pithias,* ed. Joseph Q. Adams, *Chief Pre-Shakespearean Dramas* (Cambridge, Mass., 1924).

5

Comic Evil: Marlowe to Ford

"Our prey being had, the Devil does laughing stand." --*Witch of Edmonton*, 5, 1, 77

1

THE gradual shift from a metaphysical morality of Everyman to a literal drama of One Man eventually rendered genuine tragedy possible. The tragic outcome of an action, implausible for a protagonist representing all of mankind, could and did exist for an individual hero. Elizabethan tragedy retained a morality dimension, however, resulting in a double vision of life: the world in which tragedy can and does occur is juxtaposed against a world in which tragedy may be averted. The tragic mask is a double one: the sad mask of destruction befallen a figure who is the victim of evil, and a smiling mask worn either by the agent of evil, a grinning descendant of the Vice, or by an outsider who has unwitting insight into the privative nature of evil. For Elizabethan tragedy is always concerned with evil, in a secular if not a theological context. As one critic put it, "The older Elizabethan tragedy is always moral. Macbeth or Flamineo or Vindice commits an act of sin which is the cause of the tragedy. All of the chief characters are conceived in relation to this act of sin; they are on the side of good or on the side of evil."[1]

The medieval habit of seeing a given situation from several points of view abides, offering a multiple perspective of the evil inherent in the tragic situation. The comic nature of evil finds expression in a variety of ways. The plays reveal an impressive gallery of jocular villains who wear the mantle of the Vice. In addition, comic evil appears in the form of dramaturgic contrast, either as interpolated variations on the tragic theme or as full counterpoint to the central tragic action. Essentially the substance is the same—the mockery of the world, the flesh, and the devil through exposure of their ultimate deficiency—but, in accord with the growing artfulness of the drama, it is incorporated with ever greater structural sophistication.

Nor is the comedy of evil limited to tragedy. In comic drama, through the device of dramaturgic contrast, the mockery of evil assumes the only possible counterpoint to the light-hearted central action: humorous exposure of a dark, threatening shadow. In a play primarily festive or jovial in tone, the forces of evil are often introduced as exaggeratedly serious figures—still comic although villainous and grim, but fated for scorn and amused disapprobation by the virtuous figures of the main plot. In romantic comedy in particular, a melodramatic exaggeration of evil is designed to evoke laughter, whereas in satire, where verbal humor often dominates, the denigration of evil is likely to become farcical, based on physical action or caricature.

Probably the earliest example of comic evil in Elizabethan

tragedy occurs in the works of a playwright long regarded as incapable of writing comedy—Christopher Marlowe. For years, scholars who were unaware of the thematic relevance of his comic materials strained to attribute Marlowe's comic scenes to the specific collaboration of other playwrights. Recently, however, a complete reversal of attitude has occurred, partly resulting from stage performances, such as that of *The Jew of Malta* in 1964,[2] which left its audiences exhausted by laughter, or, as one theater critic put it, the audiences laughed themselves "into a coma" over the violent scenes like the wholesale murder of the nuns in a convent. Such performances help dispel the confusion over Marlowe's "humor," which grows out of the failure to recognize its place in the early dramatic tradition of England.

Both *Doctor Faustus* and *The Jew of Malta* incorporate brilliantly original manifestations of this conventional device.[3] In *Doctor Faustus,* the tragic study of the magician who surrendered his soul to the devil, comic evil is used both in the central plot, to demonstrate the degeneration of the hero during the twenty-four years of bondage to demonic forces, and in the parallel episodes, both those involving the mock-conjurings of Wagner, a fellow student, and those of Robin and Ralph, the tavern tricksters.

Doctor Faustus's bid for superhuman power ironically leads him to the gradual loss of the high human abilities with which he was initially endowed; his debased association with the clowns, his campaign of petty trickery in the company of Mephistophilis, and his indulgence in mere horseplay, all illustrate the descent toward non-Being traditionally enacted in comic form. Embracing magic to become a god, Faustus becomes less than a man. Sacrificing his immortal soul for mortal, material power, he descends the scale of Being and is reduced to cavorting with clowns. The comedy of evil, implicit in the degeneration of the hero and necessary to his portrayal, is organically woven into the structure of the play. The disastrous consequences of yielding to deceptive evil are revealed in the increasingly comic behavior of the rapidly degenerating protagonist and, at the same time, in the increasing proportion of clownish counterpoint intruding mockingly from the lower ranges of Being in order to parody the actions of the protagonist.

The comic evidence of Faustus's deterioration occurs early in the play, when he asks Mephistophilis for a wife: "I am wanton and lascivious." The devil grants his request with a typically demonic deception. The "wife" is actually a grotesque demon—"a wife in the devil's name"—and a mock liturgical formula parodies the marriage sacrament. By the middle of the play, in the scene set in Rome, the proud scholar who once sought to attain deity is content to amuse himself with the theft of food from the Pope's well-laden table. His degenerate behavior is focused against a background reminder of his fatal alternatives—salvation and damnation—as the monks chant a catalogue of curses and a litany of saints in tense counterpoint.[4]

Even the horsecourser episode, borrowed from the Faust book and concerned with one of the most trivial and absurd tricks performed by the hero, functions integrally as an anticipation of the ultimate physical dismemberment threatening him. His flippant disposition of a limb for a practical joke appalls an audience that still recalls his equally casual disposition of his "trifle" soul.

Contrapuntal to Faustus's degenerate career is a series of farcical actions involving Wagner and the scholars in the beginning and concluding scenes and the clowns and horsecourser in the middle scenes. Wagner's mock dialectic with the students incorporates a clever parody of the main plot. His remarks are equivocal, in the manner of the Vice, as when he responds to a question about his master's whereabouts: "God in heaven knows." When Wagner conjures, the clown who is his companion, although obviously ter-

·ified, maintains his standards. Whereas Wagner condescend-ngly assumes that the clown would sell his soul for a raw houlder of mutton, the clown protests, more wisely than ne knows, that "if I pay so deere, it will be roasted and erved with a good sauce." The clown rightly fears that he night be torn to pieces by the devils, thereby foreshadowing he hero's doom. Wagner's warning is another precise antic-pation of the tragic conclusion: "Why, now sirra thou art at an houres warning whensoever or wheresoever the diuell hall fetch thee." But the clown is in no danger: he remem-pers to say "God forgive me."

Similarly, the metamorphoses in the tavern scene fore-shadow the poignant desire for transformation voiced by Faustus in the hour before his death. The clown objects to uch things on religious grounds: "How? a Christian fellow o a dogge or a catte, a mouse or a ratte?" But the moment will come when Faustus would gladly be turned into a water drop.

The Jew of Malta, which T. S. Eliot paradoxically labeled a "tragical farce," abounds in the comedy of evil. Indeed, here is little else but the humor provided by the villainous Barabas and his partner in crime, the slave Ithamore. From he moment when Barabas catalogues his heinous deeds— 'I walk abroad at night and kill sick people groaning under walls"—he deteriorates into an ever more comic figure as he and Ithamore cheerfully commit ever greater and more dia-bolically ingenious crimes. Ithamore, in fact, parodies his master's long, Vicelike confession with a detailed account of his own petty trickery:

> Once at Jerusalem, where the pilgrims kneel'd,
> I strowed powder on the Marble stones,
> And therewithall their knees would rankle, so
> That I haue laugh'd agood to see the cripples
> Goe limping home to Christendome on stilts.
>
> (ll. 973–77)

Plunging more deeply into their violent career, Ithamore and Barabas poison the Jew's own daughter Abigail along with the several nuns with whom she has lived since her conversion to Christianity. The incident provokes satirical comment on the holy orders. When Ithamore volunteers to kill the monks too, Barabas responds, "Thou shalt not need, for now the Nuns are dead,/ They'll dye with griefe" (ll. 1523–24). Later Barabas banters with the two friars who have come to convert him, one with full knowledge of the Jew's crimes, revealed to him in Abigail's dying confession. Their tacit reluctance to accuse him of crime takes a quick comic turn to fluency as they invite him to join their order when he hints that he may bequeath money to the fortunate order that wins him. Like the vices fighting among themselves, the two avaricious friars come to blows over the potential "convert."

The two friars are then grimly dispatched by means of an ingenious but farcical scheme. The first friar is killed and his body propped up against his staff: "excellent, he stands as if he were begging of Bacon" (ll. 1663–64). The second is then tricked into striking the corpse, and, feeling guilty over what he believes to be his own murderous deed, submits to punishment. Ithamore later recalls the friar's execution with gleeful satisfaction:

> I neuer knew a man take his death so patiently as this Fryar; he was ready to leape off e're the halter was about his necke; and when the Hangman had put on his Hempen Tippet, he made such haste to his prayers, as if hee had had another Cure to serue; well, goe whither he will, I'le be none of his followers in haste. (ll. 1737–43)

Ithamore's function in the play in some ways parallels that of Wagner in *Doctor Faustus.* He reflects and at the same time parodies his master's desire for gold, as Wagner does his master's desire for forbidden knowledge. And the two friars play a somewhat similar role to that of the clowns in *Doctor Faustus* in that they reflect and parody the central theme—in this case, love of gold—on still another level. The two tragic protagonists may also be seen as analogous in respect to their progressive degeneration, since each plummets rapidly from an initial grandiose aspiration to an eventual surrender to indulgence in mere horseplay. When Barabas submits to posing as a French entertainer with an absurd accent, he is as degraded as Faustus when he tricks the horsecourser. The surrender to evil is in both cases comic.

The tragedy of *Edward II* is not so rich in what is now acknowledged as Marlowe's "black humor." In one scene, however, Marlowe borrows the figure of a comic devil from the Chester mystery cycle to intensify the horrifying assassination of the king with grim diabolic humor. The assassin is named Lightbourne—an Anglicization of Lucifer—and he plans the crime with gleeful ingenuity. He laughs at the mere suggestion of relenting—"Relent! ha, ha! I use much to relent." He boasts of his professional experience:

> 'Tis not the first time I have killed a man,
> I learnde in Naples how to poison flowers,
> To strangle with a lawne thrust through the throte,
> To pierce the windpipe with a needles point,
> Or whilst one is asleepe, to take a quill
> And blowe a little powder in his eares,
> Or open his mouth, and powre quicksiluer downe.
>
> (ll. 2362–68)

When Lightbourne enters Edward's dungeon, the king asks with unwitting irony: "Who's there? What light is that?" But a close look at the intruder immediately informs the king of his intention: "Villaine, I know thou comst to murther me." Like his ancestor, this Lightbourne is given to easy tears as well as laughter, and he weeps profusely over the plight of the king. But his dissimulation is not entirel convincing, even to his nearly distraught victim. When th murder is finally achieved, Lightbourne coolly casts abou for compliments from his cohorts, Matrevis and Gurney But unlike his ancestors, the devil and the Vice, Lightbourne possesses neither mythological nor metaphorical immunity. His jaunty question, "Tell me, sirs, was it no bravelie done?" is answered by the knife of Gurney, wh stabs with quick efficiency and hastens to dispose of the bod in the moat.

Unfortunately, we shall never know the nature of thos comic episodes which were deleted by the printer from th published text of *Tamburlaine*. It seems a reasonable assumption that they too were instances of the comic natur of evil. At any rate, Marlowe, whose gift for comic writin has at last been acknowledged by some critics who recogniz his affinity with modern "black" humor, clearly demonstrate the inherited medieval convention of the "black" humor o evil.

Contemporary with Marlowe, the anonymous tragedy o *Arden of Feversham* and Kyd's *Spanish Tragedy* offer furthe examples of mirthful evil. In the grimly ironic masterpiec *Arden of Feversham,* the main comic episodes involve tw professional murderers, Black Will and Shakebag, who ar hired by the heroine, Alice, to kill her husband, Arden From the very moment that they are engaged to undertak the murder—Black Will boasting that he would kill anyon for twenty angels—the two ruffians encounter a series o comic frustrations. Each of their several futile attempts t carry out the murder becomes more ond more farcical. In their first attempt, an apprentice unwittingly closes a window on Black Will's head. On another occasion, they find themselves mistakenly locked out of Arden's house at th crucial moment chosen for entry. At still another point, th two engage in a foolish quarrel, each claiming to outdo th other in villainy. Their momentary accomplice, Greene, compares them to two dogs striving for a bone and letting a third cur steal it from them both. Even the elements conspire against them, and when they find themselves lost in a dense fog, Will aptly compares his state to hell's mouth, while Shakebag falls into a ditch. Railing in futile anger against his failure, Will indulges in the traditional boastful confesson of skillful achievements in villainy, concluding that Arden must be preserved by a miracle. Will, in fact, continually makes such ironic assertions, in the characteristic mode of evil equivocation, as when he exclaims, "And if I do not, heaven cut me off!" Once he even confirms his devilish oath by kneeling down and holding up his hands to heaven! In addition to the outrageously funny villains, moreover, *Arden* incorporates the mockery of evil continually in the subtle irony of its language, but a close analysis of the dialogue would be too extensive for inclusion here.[5]

Unlike *Arden of Feversham,* which in its entirety comments on the equivocal nature of evil, *The Spanish Tragedy,* a play more influenced by classical than by native antecedents, includes the traditional comedy of evil in only one episode.[6] That particular episode, however, so closely resembles the action involving the Vice Ill Report in *Virtuous and Godly Susanna* that one is tempted to suspect a direct influence from this late morality. In the earlier play (1568–69) about the biblical heroine, the Vice had scoffed at the possibility of his own execution only to find the fatal joke turned against him. In Kyd's tragedy, the servant named Pedringano, a partner-in-crime to the villainous Lorenzo, plays a role analogous to that of Ill Report. Pedringano's diabolic master, Lorenzo, plans to eliminate him by arranging for his execution, but the deluded servant never for a moment doubts that Lorenzo will obtain a pardon for him. While Pedringano waits cheerfully in prison, blithely ignoring the fact that his scheduled execution is approaching, a messenger boy is sent to him with a mysterious box that to all appearances contains a pardon. The boy has been forbidden to look into the box, but he cannot resist his curiosity and takes a surreptitious peek. He takes malicious delight in his new knowledge, and as a knowing observer, he chuckles over the grim joke:

> I cannot choose but smile to think how the villain will flout the gallows, scorn the audience, and descant on the hangman, and all presuming on his pardon from hence Will't not be an odd jest, for me to stand and grace every jest he makes, pointing my finger at this box, as who would say, "Mock on; here's thy warrant." Is't not a scurvy jest, that a man should jest himself to death? (3, 5, 10–17)

In the scene directly following the messenger's words Pedringano does indeed jest with the hangman, scornfully rejecting prayers offered for him on the same basis as did Ill Report: "let them alone till some other time; for now I have no great need." When the hangman offers him the halter, he responds coyly:

> O, sir, you are too forward; thou wouldst fain furnish me with a halter, to disfurnish me of my habit, so I should go out of this gear, my raiment, into that gear, the rope but hangman, now I spy your knavery, I'll not change without boot, that's flat. (3, 6, 44–48)

The deluded wretch continues his dialogue with impuden confidence:

> Ped. So then, I must up?
> Hangm. No remedy.
> Ped. Yes, but there shall be for my coming down.
> Hangm. Indeed, here's a remedy for that. (3, 6, 50–53)

Until the very moment that he dangles at the rope's end this roguish victim of illusory evil retains his firm faith in he empty box, itself a fitting symbol of nothing disguised as something.

2

In a wholly different vein from either the Senecan drama of *The Spanish Tragedy* or the passionately heroic plays of Marlowe, the works of Thomas Dekker also illustrate the persistence of the comedy of evil on the Elizabethan stage.[7] Dekker offers, in fact, a particularly useful example because of the sheer variety in his dramatic output. For purposes of the present discussion, a tragedy, a comedy, and a masque-like tragicomedy will be selected. To begin with an example of tragicomedy, *Old Fortunatus* introduces the theme of evil through both masque and iconography. The symbolic costume of the Vice is designed to suggest the deceptive nature of evil—its seeming reality and ultimate nothingness, its apparent attractiveness and actual ugliness. Vice is decribed as follows:

> Enter Vice with a gilded face, and hornes on her head; her garments long, painted before with silver halfe moones, increasing by litle and litle, till they come to the full: in the midst of them in Capitall letters this written: Crescit Evndo: her garment painted behind with fooles faces and divels heads: and underneath it in the midst this written, Ha, Ha, He. (1, 3)

Lest the iconography not be sufficiently clear, Dekker places an interpretation in a sermonlike speech by the character of Fortune:

> for they whose soules
> Still revell in the nights of vanitie,
> On the faire cheekes of Vice still fixe their eye.
> Because her face doth shine, and all her bosome
> Beares silver Moones, thou wast enamord of her.

But hadst thou upward lookt, and seene these shames,
Or viewed her round about, and in this glasse
Seene Idiots faces, heads of devils and hell,
And read this ha, ha, he, this merrie storie,
Thou wouldst have loathd her: where, by loving her,
Thou bearst this face, and wearst this ugly head,
And if shee once can bring thee to this place,
Lowd sounds these ha, ha, he, sheele laugh apace.

(4, 1, 172–84

Nor does the homiletic figure of Vice itself remain silen
about her methods of operation:

If my Angelicall and Saint-like forme
Can win some amorous foole to wanton here,
And taste the fruite of this alluring tree,
Thus shall his sawcie browes adorned bee,
To make us laugh.

(1, 3, 90–94

In the action of the play the influence of the Vice on hi
human victims serves to illustrate further the absurdity o
insubstantial evil. In one scene, for example, Andelocia
the younger son of the titular hero and heir to his magi
purse, becomes transformed into a merry fool simply b
being in the presence of the Vice. Within the sphere of evi
influence, he laughs wildly, comments foolishly, and delight
in the discomfiture of others, calling for further cruelty t
incite further irresponsible mirth. The Vice also mislead
the young men named Longaville and Montrose by para
doxically setting them free from punishment for their crime
With wry humor, he notes that freedom for them will b
suffering.

Be gon, but you in libertie shall find

More bondage than in chaines, fooles, get you hence,
Both wander with tormented conscience.

(5, 2, 248–50)

But in this moral masque, Vice is eventually defeated by the bright beauty of Virtue, also cast as a personified abstraction in symbolic dress.

Dekker also employs comic evil in his popular tragedy *The Witch of Edmonton,* written in collaboration with Ford and Rowley. In this "tragicomical" play, the perversity of evil operates through trickery and equivocation on both of the serious levels of action involving the protagonist, Frank Thorney, and the witch, and on the comic level of the clown, Cuddy Banks. In all three actions the medium of evil is Tom, a "familiar" in the shape of a dog. Urged on by the dog to criminal behavior, Frank murders Susan, to whom he is bound in a bigamous marriage. Also with the aid of the black dog, Mother Sawyer, the witch, achieves her revenge against a young woman who is driven to suicide. On the comic level, however, trickery results in temporary reversals and the limited privation is safely subject to laughter. Young Cuddy, the clownish lover, agrees to follow the canine "familiar," who has promised to lead him to the charming Kate, with whom he is in love. The black dog seemingly leads him to the rendezvous he desires, for he sees what appears to be Kate but in reality is a spirit resembling her. When the clown tries to embrace his phantom beloved, he tumbles into a bog, becoming very wet and disillusioned in his romantic ambitions. The canine then reproaches him with the sort of equivocal avowal so characteristic of the Vice—"Take heed how thou trustest the Devil another time." When the clown recognizes the demonic nature nature of the dog, he rejects it, as does the good man who becomes aware of the merely privative nature of the evil that seems to offer such substantial temptations. When the dog further asserts the Luciferian position—"These that are joys denied, must take delight/ In sins and mischiefs, 'tis the Devils right"—Cuddy, with blunt, innocent faith, defies the argument, adding amusingly, "The Devil you can."

The comic nature of privative evil can be exposed in a primarily comic play as well as in tragedy. In Dekker's comedy *Westward Ho,* written in collaboration with Webster, a moment of sudden comic revelation betrays the ugliness of sinful lust. The moment occurs to the protagonist, the Earl, who breathlessly anticipates the night of his assignation with a married woman. He is well aware of his guilt, which he admits freely, but condones it as an inevitable consequence of his animal nature.

> This, the strong Magick of our appetite:
> To feast which richly, life it selfe undoes,
> Who'd not die thus?
>
> (4, 2, 33–34)

And he confirms his appetites, vowing through his lust to "turn her into a devil, whom I adore."

> Tis but a minute's pleasure, and the sin
> Scarce acted is repented: shun it than:
> O, he that can abstain is more than man!
> Tush! Resolvs't thou to do ill: be not precise.
> Who write of virtue best, are slaves to vice.
>
> (4, 2, 46–50)

The revelation of the "reality" of evil is a very funny fulfillment of the would-be seducer's intention to turn his mistress into a devil. When he bids her remove her mask, he discovers the person of her husband, who has donned her clothes. The sight of a male visage is a hilarious shock:

> I am abus'd, deluded: Speak what are thou?
> Ud's death, speak, or I'll kill thee. In that habit
> I look'd to find an angel, but thy face
> Shows thou'rt a Devil.
>
> (4, 2, 61–64)

The context is farcical, but the venerable message is serious.

The dramatic world of John Marston is less genial than that of Dekker.[8] Predominantly satirical in tone, Marston's plays are all didactically concerned with the exposure of evil, with laughter at the insubstantiality of evil being only one of his several techniques to achieve that exposure. In one of his best plays, *The Dutch Courtesan,* the comic dimension of evil is contrapuntally portrayed. The main plot concerns the cruelly treacherous courtesan, Franceschina, and her almost successful attempt to have her unfaithful lover murdered. The subplot involves the equally treacherous but less dangerous and infinitely funnier intrigue perpetrated by Cocledemoy against the tavern-keeper, Mulligrub. Cocledemoy, a Vicelike trickster, is completely unmotivated. Unlike the rejected courtesan plotting revenge, he deals in evil simply because it is his nature to do so, and the unhappy Mulligrub is his chosen victim. Cocledemoy first contrives to "shave" the unfortunate man (even as Grim the Collier had been doubly shaved in *Damon and Pithias*). Next he plots to steal his most valuable goblets. Then he tricks Mulligrub into being dragged off to prison, accused of theft and of keeping a bawdy house. But eventually the rascally Cocledemoy is threatened with hanging, and he asserts his innocence, impenitently bidding the much-gulled taverner to think of his own "sins and iniquities." Naturally he escapes such a dire fate, for all that he has done has been only "euphoniae gratis," but the vicious Franceschina is sent off to prison.

The flavor of Cocledemoy's language is worth savoring:

> Were I to bite an honest gentleman, a poor grogaran poet, or a penurious parson that had but ten pigs' tails in a twelve-month, and, for want of learning, had but one good stool in a fortnight, I were damned beyond the works of supererrogation! But to wring the withers of my gouty, barm'd spigot-frigging jumbler of elements, Mulligrub, I hold it as lawful as sheepe-shearing, taking eggs from hens, caudles from asses, or butter'd shrimps from horses—they make no use of them, were not provided for them. (3, 2, 33–42)

The world of Marston's *Malcontent,* the corrupt and decadent court of Genoa, is almost wholly evil. A satiric tragedy *manqué,* the play concerns four murders but contains no corpses. Both plot and characters embody the theme of fraudulent and deficient evil. The Machiavellian villain is outwitted by a youthful courtier; the court bawd peddles her possets and recites her unsavory recipes for beautification to a lovely young woman who has no need for them; the usurping Duke, not a bad sort at heart, is twice the theoretical victim of plots to destroy him. The conventional "fatal revels" scene that ends the play quite unconventionally culminates in multiple unmasking rather than multiple murder.

Above all, the fact that the protagonist, the deposed Duke Altofronto, plays an assumed role throughout most of the play, is in keeping with the theme of a deceptive society. Altofronto poses as the malcontent, Malevole, "one of the most prodigious affections that ever convers'd with nature: a man, or rather a monster, more discontent than Lucifer when he was thrust out of the presence . . ." (1, 3, 16–19). Malevole rails against the society that condones him by allotting him the freedom of a licensed jester. His scathing honesty is as much out of tune with the court as is the "vilest out-of-tune music" that heralds his appearance on stage in the opening scene. His railing is at once bitter and funny, grim and gay. He defends his nobility ironically:

> Sure I am of noble kind; for I find myself possessed with all their qualities: love dogs, dice, and drabs; scorn wit in stuff-clothes; have beat my shoemaker, knock'd my seamstress, cuckold' my 'pothecary, and undone my tailor. Noble! Why not? (3, 3, 52–56)

He scoffs at religion:

> I have seen seeming Piety change her robe so oft that sure none but some arch-devil can shape her a new petticoat. (1, 3, 10–12)

And he scorns the world:

> World! 'Tis the only region of death, the greatest shop of the devil, the cruel'st prison of men, out of the which none can pass without paying their dearest breath for a fee. (4, 4, 26–28)

In such a world, the idealism of an Altofronto can survive only through the grinning mask of "gross-jawed" Malevole. The refusal to compromise with corruption is the prerogative only of a jesting malcontent. The exchange between Malevole and the chameleon courtier Bilioso epitomizes the mood of the play:

Bilioso: We must collogue sometimes, forswear sometimes.
Malevole: Be damn'd sometimes.
Bilioso: Right!/ . . . No man can be honest at all hours.

(5, 3, 75–79)

A play somewhat similar in mood is Chapman's last comedy, *The Widow's Tears.*[9] Here again the comic image of evil is projected against the background of a topsy-turvy world. Tharsalio, the cynical hero of the play, rejects the goddesses of both Virtue and Fortune in favor of his own chosen deity, Confidence. The bases of his worship are his own energetic but amoral "virtu" and the moral weakness of the rest of humanity. With the help of Confidence, he triumphs in his first enterprise, the wooing of the wealthy widow Eudora. He conquers the haughty and unapproachable widow through audacity and a shamelessly direct appeal to her lust. Then, confirmed in his view that widows' tears are hypocritical and transitory, he goes on to test his sister-in-law, Cynthia, renowned as a paragon of chastity. His testing method is as cruel as confident. He persuades his brother to fake death in order to observe the reaction of his supposed widow. In obviously genuine grief, Cynthia retires to her husband's tomb, in the company of her servant. There, after several days of fasting, weak in body and in spirit, the widow yields to the advances of a man dressed as a soldier, whom she believes to be her husband's murderer but who is actually her husband in disguise. Tharsalio becomes euphoric when he discovers the pair, and dances in unabashed celebration of her fall. The triumph of energetic evil over exhausted virtue is expressed in mirth and music.

But the final vision of evil does not rest either in the cynical hero or in the degenerate heroine. In the final scene of the play, where according to the conventions of Elizabethan comedy a restoration of order should take place, exactly the reverse occurs. The conclusion of the play is a parody of justice, a paradigm of disorder. The civil authority who appears on the scene to take charge is the foolish governor, who was raised to that seat of honor by "bribing courtiers." The Captain comments bitterly:

> Well, my mind must stoop to his high place,
> And learn within itself to sever him from that,
> And to adore Authority the Goddess,

> However borne by an unworthy beast;
> And let the beast's dull apprehension take
> The honor done to Isis, done to himself.
>
> (5, 1, 148–53)

When the "beast" is introduced, we recognize the familiar iconography of the Vice:

> Room for a strange Governor. The perfect draught of a most brainless, imperious upstart. O desert! Where wert thou when this wooden dagger was gilded over with the title of Governor? (5, 1, 557–60)

And, as he prepares to speak, Tharsalio aptly and ironically comments:

> All wisdom be silent; now speaks authority. (5, 1, 562)

The Governor's speeches, foolish and perverse, are interrupted by mocking asides of Tharsalio, who finally remarks,

> Nay, the Vice must snap his authority at all he meets; how shall't else be known what part he plays? (5, 1, 610–11)

The Governor announces his mandate of perversion: "I'll turn all topsy-turvy," fulfilling both the specific remark of the soldier made earlier, to the effect that "in this topsy-turvy world friendship and bosom-kindness are but made covers for mischief," and the general atmosphere of the play, the fallen world of satire, the grimly comic world of privative evil.

3

In the early years of the seventeenth century, the time of *The Malcontent* and *The Widow's Tears,* the genres of tragedy and comedy tended to lose their distinction and merge in the direction of irony and satire. Similarly, good and evil were no longer presented in terms of a clear-cut, black-and-white opposition. Consequently, for a brief time, the comedy of evil was no longer channeled into counterpoint or variations on a theme, but was permitted to overflow the entire world of a play. In a few brilliant plays the precarious balance between the "Elizabethan world picture" and "Jacobean disorder" is maintained only through a total perspective of comic evil.

In this moment of transition, the easy assurance of the old laughter, fortified by theology, is gone, yet the new secular vision, which must reject metaphysical laughter, is not yet born. At this moment of *mannerist* tension the surrender to evil makes everything seem funny, yet, by the same token, nothing is really funny for want of a fixed point of reference. In art the portrayal of a demonic, fallen world is not matched by a corresponding view of the serene angelic order just above; hence the laughter is often hollow and unsettling. Consequently a play like *The Revenger's Tragedy* is either all comic or not comic at all, depending on whether one's sense of evil is basically medieval or modern.[10]

The Revenger's Tragedy vividly depicts an overwhelmingly evil world through an ironically comic perspective. The morality elements that provide the conventional superstructure of this powerful play are traditional but the moral absolutes that they imply are poised precariously on a razor's edge of paradox, double-entendre, and unremitting irony. The complex protagonist, Vindice, capers from one disguise to another, now hero, now villain, now melancholy scholar, now Vice. And the providential thunder that sounds in response to his summons dies away, lost in the schism between divine intervention and demonic mockery.

The play opens with a candlelit pageant of the deadly sins, cast as members of a corrupt court. In the role of moral commentator, Vindice—while clutching the skull of his murdered mistress—bitterly bemoans both the corruption at court and the ultimate corruption, mortality.

He addresses the "shell of death" in a homiletic soliloquy that includes the grimly humorous pun: "When two heaven-pointed diamonds were set/ In those unsightly rings." But he soon subdues his moral outrage sufficiently to agree to play the pander to Lussurioso, a role that proves to be the first step in his degeneration. He assumes the part by making a Vicelike confession of past villainies:

> I have been witness to the surrenders of a thousand virgins, and not so little. I have seen patrimonies washed a-pieces, fruit fields turned into bastards. (1, 3, 50–52)

As the role of Vice becomes more and more part and parcel of his nature, Vindice indulges in ironic asides to the audience and relates his plans for vengeance with unquenchable cheerfulness. Enjoying the many ironies inherent in his role, he gleefully explains to his brother at a crucial point in the action: "I'm hired to kill myself!"

When Vindice plans his masterpiece—dressing up the skeleton of his betrothed to lure the lustful Duke to his death—his wit sparkles grimly:

> Here's an eye,
> Able to tempt a great man—to serve God;
> A pretty hanging lip, that has forgot now to dissemble:
> Methinks this mouth should make a swearer tremble,
> A drunkard clasp his teeth, and not undo 'em
> To suffer wet damnation to run through 'em.
>
> (3, 5, 54–59)

And as he retires with his brother to lie in wait for the Duke, he instructs Hippolyto: "Brother, fall you back/ a little, with the bony lady" (3, 5, 120–21)

With each step in his revenge, Vindice becomes more jocular. The scene in which he carries out Lussurioso's orders to murder Piato—his own assumed role—is broadly comic. Not only is the situation itself amusing in its irony, since Piato was the name Vindice himself assumed in disguise, but now the identity has been transferred through garments to the corpse of the Duke, whom Vindice has already murdered. When he has convinced Lussurioso that the supposed "Piato" is lying on the ground dead drunk, the banter about his murder follows accordingly:

> Vindice. Shall we kill him now he's drunk?
> Lussurioso. Ay, best of all.
> Vindice. Why, then he will ne'er live
> To be sober.
> Lussurioso. No matter, let him reel to hell.
> Vindice. But being so full of liquor, I fear he will
> Put out all the fire--
> Lussurioso. Thou art a mad beast.
> Vindice. [Aside] And leave none to warm our lordship's golls withal.—[Aloud] For he that dies drunk falls into hell-fire like a bucket o' water, qush, qush. (5, 1, 43–51)

But Vindice agrees to stab the corpse, a deed that Lussurioso acknowledges as nimbly done. When he then discovers that the body is in reality that of his dead father, he cries out "Villains! murderers!" But Vindice's reaction is flippant: "That's a jest." And when Lussurioso logically blames the missing Piato for the crime, since the corpse is wearing his clothing, Vindice only remarks frivolously, "O rascal! Was he not asham'd/ To put the duke into a greasy doublet?" (5, 1, 65–66).

As in the case of his ancestral Vices, Vindice's humorous pursuit of crime eventually overreaches itself, and the revenger who enjoyed his revenge with such zest is finally hoist by his own petard. He cannot resist boasting to Antonio that his dispatch of the Duke was "somewhat witty carried," and that elderly man, who has newly assumed the Duke's role, quickly dispatches him for proper justice.

> You, that would murder him, would murder me. (5, 3, 103)

The final irony in Vindice's career is that he has fulfilled his evil mission, the one to which he was assigned by Lussurioso: "I'm hired to kill myself!" The equivocal truth of evil has rebounded upon the speaker.

The comic treatment of evil in the play is by no means limited to the role of Vindice. Since the world of the play is evil, the stream of comedy flows through most of the dialogue and episodes. The episode involving the death sentence of the Duchess's younger son, for example, resorts to a conventional formula, repeating the Pedringano incident in *The Spanish Tragedy*. Sentenced to death for committing rape on Antonio's wife, the imprisoned youth has just read a letter from his two brothers that he interprets as a promise of rescue. He challenges the officers who come to lead him to execution:

> Junior Bro. Look you officious whoresons, words of comfort: "Not long a prisoner."
> 1st Off. It says true in that, sir, for you must suffer presently.
> Junior Bro. A villainous Duns upon the letter, knavish exposition! Look you then here, sir: "We'll get thee out by a trick," says he.
> 2nd Off. That may hold too, sir, for you know a trick is commonly four cards, which was meant by us four officers. (3, 4, 56–62)

Not only is the younger son thus executed through equivocal language, but he also goes to his own death echoing the tritest of Jacobean puns: "I die for that which every woman loves."

In the brilliantly theatrical fifth act, a conventional "fatal revels" concludes the action of this play-long Dance of Death.[11] The mood of Gothic humor is introduced in the last scene of the third act by the stunned Ambitioso, who has just learned that his attempt to save the younger son has failed. He comments, "I see now, there's nothing sure in mortality, but mortality" (3, 6, 89–90). In the final scene, the very moment before the Masque of revengers, Lussurioso ironically praises the flattering noble who outdoes his cohorts in wishing long life to the new ruler: "But 'tis my hope, my lord, you shall ne'er die" (5, 3, 34). A few lines later, the four masquers stab the four seated at the table, celebrating the installation of the new Duke. Vindice, delighting in his successful revenge, whispers his guilt in the ears of the dying Duke, adding mockingly, "Tell nobody." But Vindice proceeds to overreach himself when he confesses his crime openly to the new ruler, the elderly Antonio. The deed was, to be sure, "somewhat witty carried," but Antonio does not respond with a jest.

A comic tone pervades this latter-day morality,[12] not only in Vindice's mordant irony but in the nervous, sardonic dialogue and in the mocking hyperbole of venerable stage conventions. Even the most violent episodes are grotesquely humorous, as when Vindice and his brother stand over the prostrate figure of the Duke, with sword on his tongue, forcing him to watch the adultery-incest of his wife. More than almost any other play of its time, *The Revenger's Tragedy* appeals to a modern audience aware of the "gallows humor" convention, which is the twentieth-century postscript to comic evil.

The uneasy equilibrium achieved in *The Revenger's Tragedy* does not reappear in English drama. Only a desiccated tradition survives in the muted pattern of the late-Jacobean stage. Modern scholars who are not sufficiently aware of the traditional comedy of evil have been particularly baffled by this vestigial manifestation of comic tone in late-

Jacobean tragedy. Recently a scholar has written of Webster's *Duchess of Malfi,* "The confusion in *The Duchess of Malfi* seems to me to arise from an injudicious mixing of, and a failure to integrate, the comic and satiric elements. These elements are so pronounced as to weaken, if not destroy, the tragic effect."[13] The role of Bosola appears to be a failure for the same reason: "The comic spirit that pervades his roles as revenger and as tool villain is in conflict with his development as a tragic character." Viewed in a historical perspective, however, the plays of Webster are between those of Tourneur, which represent a point of no return for the venerable Gothic mockery of evil, and those of John Ford, in which the dramaturgic technique has become divorced from the underlying ethic that engendered it.

The remarkable tenacity of the comic demonstration of evil is, however, manifested in the mere fact of Ford's insistence on trying to incorporate it, however unsuccessfully.[14] In his early play called *Love's Sacrifice* Ford attempted to devote a subplot to the exposure of deficient evil. The love theme in the main plot concerns the tragically adulterous but admirably noble relationship between the aristocratic Fernando and the chaste Bianca, wife to the Duke. Their genuine and honorable love is parodied in the subplot through the illicit amours of the courtier Ferentes. This wanton gentleman, engaged in decidedly unplatonic affairs, succeeds in making three of his mistresses pregnant, then refuses to marry any of them. This supposedly funny parallel is precipitously brought to a violent end a mere two scenes after its introduction. In this climactic scene, the dastardly courtier and the three victims of his lust appear disguised as players in a court masque. Dancing a demonic ballet, the masked ladies surround their mutual seducer and jointly stab him to death. Obviously the same "fatal revels" tradition shapes this scene as it did the superficially analogous scene in *The Revenger's Tragedy,* but the profound irony rooted in genuine metaphysical laughter is missing in Ford's use of the device. Even granting Ford's possible inability to write effective comedy, it is obvious that the scene fails because the evil involved is not evil in the philosophical sense of non-Being. The meaningful definition of evil that gave symbolic import to the earlier masques of murder is here lacking. As a result, the ballet of death is form without substance—like a modern maypole dance.

Once more, in *Tis Pity She's A Whore,* Ford introduces a contrapuntal comedy of evil. Once again the attempt falls short of success. In this play the moral lines of force are ambiguous from the start. The technical formula involves contrasting the noble love of the hero and heroine with the absurd love of the foolish clown for the heroine. The contrast is strained, however, because the noble love is in fact incestuous, and the comic love is in fact sincere. As a result, while the reader finds himself responding with decided ambivalence toward Annabella and her brother, Giovanni, he also finds himself responding with at least sympathy, if not downright admiration, for the poor, ill-fated suitor, Bergetto. The confused response is heightened in Bergetto's death scene. The unfortunate fool is mistaken for someone else as he hastens to a midnight tryst and is therefore stabbed to death by Grimaldi, another suitor to Annabella. Since Grimaldi is a villainous figure, and since the world of suitors that surrounds Annabella is corrupt and ugly, Bergetto becomes a disastrously pathetic character in his moment of death. Although he dies uttering a foolish obscenity, the attempt at comedy is rendered purposeless and painful.

In his final tragedy, Ford abandoned the contrapuntal comedy of evil, which for him had deteriorated into mere comic relief. In the Prologue to *The Broken Heart* he firmly rejects the convention that he had before so superficially accepted. He states unequivocally that this play will not contain "jests fit for a brothel" and that no "apish laughter" will be introduced to detract from the seriousness of the tragedy. Ironically, in this assertion Ford is admitting his complete break with the Christian tradition. He has even forgotten that laughter is not "apish": man is by definition "homo risus capax."

It seems fitting, then, to conclude this discussion of comic evil on the Jacobean stage by considering Jonson's delightful parody of it in *The Devil Is An Ass.*[15] It was of course inevitable that such a familiar and solidly established dramatic convention would be honored obliquely through parody as well as directly through imitation. Jonson's play, written in 1616, opens with an iambic pentameter line of "Hoh hoh's" spoken by Satan. Perhaps this is the most succinct statement of the comedy of evil yet uttered. As the play proceeds, the minor devil Pug requests permission to travel to earth in order to advance the hellish cause on that planet. He wants also to take along a Vice as his companion in deviltry. The Vice Iniquity appears in response to his summons, reciting doggerel verse about his mission:

What is he, calls vpon me, and would seeme to lack a Vice?
Ere his words be halfe spoken, I am with him in a trice;
Here, there, and euerywhere, as the Cat is with the mice:
True *vetus Iniquitas.*

(1, 1, 44–47)

In the course of the action that follows, the devil and Vice are worsted by their more sophisticated human counterparts, and poor Pug is led to lament that "Hell is a grammar-school compared to this!" The infernal aid of both Satan and Iniquity is necessary to save him from being hanged—in the very body of the hanged criminal, which he had borrowed for clothing his demonic spirit in the first place! Throughout the play, the action is enlivened with the motif of devilish laughter, sometimes imitated by depraved humanity, as when the young gallant Fitzdottrell feigns demonic possession.

Jonson's parody is an affectionate one, however, and its gentle mockery did not mean that stage devils—and villains—ceased to make asses of themselves in subsequent Jacobean drama. But there was no question that the venerable comic romp with the forces of evil had lost much of its real meaning by the 1620s. The metaphysical implications that brought about the comedy of evil and sustained it so centrally in Christian art and literature had virtually faded away by the second decade of the seventeenth century.

Notes to Chapter 5

1. Lord David Cecil, *Poets and Story-Tellers* (Indianapolis, Ind., 1964).
2. See Nicholas Brooke, "Marlowe the Dramatist," in *Elizabethan Theatre,* ed. J. R. Brown and B. Harris (London, 1966).
3. Christopher Marlowe, *Works,* ed. C. F. Tucker Brooke (Oxford, 1910).
4. See Nan Carpenter, "Music in Dr. Faustus," *Notes and Queries* 195 (1950): 180–81.
5. *Arden of Feversham,* ed. J. S. Cunningham, New Mermaid Series (London, 1970).
6. Thomas Kyd, *The Spanish Tragedy,* ed. Philip Edwards (London, 1959).
7. *The Dramatic Works of Thomas Dekker,* ed. Fredson Bowers, 4 vols. (Cambridge, 1953–61), vols. 1–4.
8. In the absence of a recent collected edition of the plays of John Marston, the best editions of the single plays are those in the University of Nebraska's Regents Renaissance Drama series: *The Dutch Courtesan,* ed. M. L. Wine (Lincoln, Neb., 1965); *The Malcontent,* ed. M. L. Wine (1964).
9. George Chapman, *The Widow's Tears,* ed. Ethel Smeak (Lincoln, Neb., 1964).
10. Cyril Tourneur, *The Revenger's Tragedy,* ed. R. A. Foakes (London, 1966).

11. See Samuel Schoenbaum, "The Revenger's Tragedy: Jacobean Dance of Death," *Modern Language Quarterly* 15 (1954) : 201–7.
12. See L. G. Salinger, "The Revenger's Tragedy and the Morality Tradition," *Scrutiny* 11 (March 1938) : 402–24. *The Revenger's Tragedy* was performed at Amherst College in February 1967, probably for the first time in the United States. Among the striking features of this excellent performance were the emphasis on the morality features of the play and the bold exploitation of the comic vein. No attempt was made to disguise the symbolic morality characterization with anachronistic naturalism. The Gothic humor of the skull scenes and the incisive wit in many of Vindice's speeches were underscored with great success. The audience's need to laugh was thus directly absorbed, whereas a straight-faced, "heavy" performance would have evoked the incompatible laughter that inevitably greets melodrama.
13. See J. M. Luecke, "The Duchess of Malfi: Comic and Satiric Confusion in Tragedy," *SEL* 4 (1964) : 275–90.
14. In the absence of a modern collected edition of John Ford's plays, I have used the New Mermaid Series editions of *The Broken Heart*, ed. Brian Morris (New York, 1965) and *Tis Pity She's A Whore*, ed. Brian Morris (New York, 1968) . *For Love's Sacrifice*, however, I used the edition of Ford's dramatic works edited by W. Bang and Henry de Vocht, 2 vols. (Louvain, 1908) .
15. *Ben Jonson*, ed. C. H. Herford and Percy Simpson, 11 vols. (Oxford, 1925–52) , 6.

6
Shakespeare and the Comedy of Evil

"Not one now to mock your own grinning?"
-- *Hamlet*, 5, 1, 180

1

LIKE his contemporaries, Shakespeare was concerned with dramatizing the moral conflict of good and evil; like them, he also exploited the traditional comedy of evil, a dramatic convention that he probably first encountered in Stratford when as a boy he watched the performances of moral plays, still popular at that time.[1] Not all of his plays draw upon this convention, and among those which do there is a vast range of treatment and emphasis. Perhaps the only valid generalization about Shakespeare's scattered and various dramatizations of comic evil is that he stressed verbal over physical humor. His comic villains, for example, typically display the attributes of perversion and negation and demonstrate the techniques of equivocation and mockery; they rarely betray the grotesque and obscene dimensions of evil. Shakespeare's "miserific" vision is more diabolic than bestial.

That Shakespeare accepted—at least for dramatic purposes—the theological definition of evil as non-Being is most obvious in *Macbeth*,[2] a profoundly Christian play that explores the nature of evil and the tragic consequences of surrender to its illusory appeal. Informing the moral world of the play with an almost Dantesque explicitness is a vision of the equivocal nature of evil and its double-dealing results. Macbeth is portrayed in suspense between the options of good and evil. The evil he chooses does not remove its deceptive veil until the moment of his death. When he finally becomes aware of the utter negation implicit in his choice, he is already in hell in this world, even if he could "jump the life to come."

The theme of evil's reversal of values is introduced with the first appearance of the weird sisters. "Fair is foul and foul is fair," they chant, establishing not only the murky Dis-like atmosphere of the play, but also, and more important, the symbolism of an equivocal evil. These foul emissaries of evil seem fair to Macbeth because of their promises, but such fairness graced as well the kiss of Judas, the snowy complexion of Spenser's false Florimell, and the brightness of the newly fallen Lucifer. Although Banquo suspects the fraudulent motives beneath the "honest trifles" they speak, Macbeth is content to rest in the illusion that "nothing is but what is not." The confirming consequences of the witches' first prediction operate through falseness. The Thane of Cawdor, "a gentleman on whom [Duncan] built an absolute trust," dies a traitor, leaving his title and the king's confidence to the latter's "peerless kinsman," Macbeth (1, 4).

The witches' words, reverberating with duplicity throughout the play, are echoed in the acts of nature, which reverses itself as if twisted in the grip of human manifestations of evil. The day becomes dark as the night; tame horses turn wild and break from their stalls; and an owl hawks a falcon. The evil that masquerades as good also affects the self-knowledge of human beings, at a loss to distinguish the true. "We do not know ourselves," complains Ross, and even Scotland, sundered by the political evil of disorder, is "afraid to know itself." Macbeth, having made his dark choice, decides it were best not to know himself.

Macbeth also fails to realize that the commitment to evil distorts immediately as well as destroying ultimately the good of the intellect. His soul anticipates its destiny as he hardens past the possibility of repentance, becoming rigid, silent, and cold: inhuman in his further crimes, untouched by his wife's death, and bitter about the apparent meaninglessness of life itself. Pursuing profit and glory that prove to be phantoms, Macbeth at the same time fails to realize that the promises of evil are ambiguous and its rewards equivocal. He awakens to the lie of evil only after his disillusionment as to its earthly compensations. Too late, he discovers that the devil "lies like truth" when the misleading words of the witches are exposed in the spectacle of the moving forest and in the revelation of Macduff's unnatural birth. Like the witches themselves, their glowing predictions, which "seemed corporal, melted." His battle won and lost, Macbeth acknowledges a barren sceptre in his grip. The brief throne and brief candle signify punishment in both worlds. The eternal jewel is not bartered for earthly gain; it is spent for nothing.

Betrayed in deepest consequence, Macbeth recognizes evil as delusion. His warning comment is deeply rooted in medieval theology, which defined evil as non-Being:

> And be these juggling fiends no more believed,
> That palter with us in a double sense;

> That keep the word of promise to our car,
> And break it to our hope.
>
> (5, 8, 19–22)

The Old Man, who pronounces a blessing on those who turn bad to good, might have added, in keeping with the same tradition, "damned be those who, according to the very nature of evil, pervert the good."

But this delineation of evil, though Christian, is scarcely comic. This is not to say, however, that *Macbeth* is an exception to the conventionally comic portrayal of privative evil. On the contrary, for a brief but brilliant moment, in a scene of almost infinite implications, comic evil takes the stage in the person of the porter at the gate.[3] As he quite self-consciously assumes the familiar role of devil-porter, reverberations from the Harrowing of Hell episodes in the mystery cycles intensify every word he speaks. As he answers the ominous knock, he mutters, "If a man were porter of hell gate, he should have old turning the key." But whereas in the cyclic plays the porter opened the gates to Jesus, who entered hell in order to rout the blustering demons and rescue the Old Testament prophets, here he opens to Macduff and Lennox, who enter the hell of Macbeth's own making. The porter then cites Beelzebub, one of the demons who appeared in the Harrowing of Hell episodes, but drunkenly forgets the "other devil's name." Meanwhile he prates of equivocation,[4] the diabolic mode of discourse, with heavy irony: "Faith, here's an equivocator, that could swear in both the scales against either scale; who committed treason enough for God's sake, yet could not equivocate to heaven." The application to Macbeth, who realizes that he cannot equivocate to heaven, is obvious enough. Equally fitting to Macbeth, albeit in a different way, is the remark that "this place is too cold for Hell." Surely Macbeth, traitor to kinsman, guest, and lord, would deserve damnation in the frozen lake of Dante's ninth circle.[5]

Macduff engages in a brief colloquy with the porter that comically demonstrates the equivocal procedures of evil. The porter announces first that "drink is a great provoker of three things . . . nose-painting, sleep, and urine." But in contrast, he goes on to explain that drink equivocates with lechery. "Lechery, sir, it provokes and unprovokes; it provokes the desire, but it takes away the performance: therefore much drink may be said to be an equivocator with lechery: it makes him and it mars him; it sets him on and it takes him off; it persuades him and disheartens him; makes him stand to and not stand to; in conclusion, equivocates him in a sleep, and giving him the lie, leaves him." The comic irony of such equivocation applies directly to Macbeth's experiences with the prophetic evil of the witches. Just as drink rewards the lecher only with "the lie," so the kingship grants Macbeth the very reverse of the power and glory that he had expected and for which he had forfeited his soul. As J. Middleton Murry noted long ago, Macbeth "is become the instrument of the equivocation of the fiend that lies like truth." The amusing episode of the devil-porter symbolically confirms Macbeth's surrender to demonic equivocation.[6]

Although the porter scene is the only comedy in *Macbeth,* the play serves as a useful touchstone for the configuration of privative evil that underlies many comic moments in Shakespeare's other Christian plays. His Roman plays are, of course, exceptional in that he retains there, for the most part, a historical fidelity to humanistic rather than theological values. In the world of *Antony and Cleopatra,* for example, the terms *good* and *evil* are meaningless. But in the Christian plays moral evil is depicted quite consistently as a reversal or negation of the good.

2

One dimension of Shakespeare's involvement with comic

evil is his use of comic techniques to represent criminality. The craftiness and ingenuity of several of his criminal figures are manifested with a zesty good humor. This sense of sport and fun, which characterizes the villainy of Aaron the Moor, for example, has led at least one critic to speak of his "perverse sense of humor." But several of Shakespeare's blackest villains are virtuosos in their art, dedicated to the endless pleasure of the game, and alarmingly witty in their frank verbal revelations of technique. At times their horrendous deeds are almost overshadowed by the double meanings, mocking asides, paronomasia, and miscellaneous wordplay with which they cheerfully commit them. But it is not the humor that is perverse: evil by definition is humorous in its perversity.

The tragedy of *Richard III* offers several examples of nimble-witted villains jesting through performance of their crimes. The scene involving the jocular quibbling of the two hired murderers is classic in its configuration of comic criminality. Commissioned by the Duke of Gloucester to do away with his brother Clarence in the tower, the murderers are downright gleeful as they discuss possible ways of committing the crime. When the first murderer announces to the lieutenant of the tower his intention to see the imprisoned Clarence, he borrows a formula from Titivillus: "I would speak with Clarence, and I came hither on my legs."[7] Left alone then with their sleeping victim, the murderers frivolously debate procedure:

> Second Murderer. What, shall we stab him as he sleeps?
> First Murderer. No, he'll say 'twas done cowardly when he wakes.
> Second Murderer. Why, he shall never wake until the great Judgment Day.
> First Murderer. Why, then he'll say we stabbed him sleeping. (1, 4, 100–107)

Mention of judgment day begins to breed remorse in the

second murderer, but only momentarily, as remorse in turn yields to thoughts of reward:

> First Murderer. How dost thou feel thyself now?
> Second Murderer. Faith, some certain dregs of conscience are yet within me.
> First Murderer. Remember our reward when the deed's done.
> Second Murderer. Zounds, he dies! I had forgot the reward.
> First Murderer. Where is thy conscience now?
> Second Murderer. O, in the Duke of Gloucester's purse. (1, 4, 121–27)

Resolute once more, he merrily accepts and augments the suggestion of his cohort:

> First Murderer. Take him on the costard with the hilts of thy sword, and then throw him into the malmsey butt in the next room.
> Second Murderer. O excellent device! And make a sop of him. (1, 4, 156–60)

During this scene the conversation of the two murderers offers a kind of verbal parallel to the leering faces of the torturers in Gothic paintings of the crucifixion, as, for example, those of the German artist Grünewald.

Comic manipulation of language is also one of the favorite techniques of the major as well as the minor criminals of the piece. When Lord Hastings has been singled out by Richard as his next victim, the lords Buckingham and Catesby both indulge in humorous equivocation. Taunting Hastings for his serene overconfidence, Catesby assures him that "The Princes both make high account of you," but adds in an aside, "For they account his head upon the bridge." Similarly Buckingham, quite aware that Hastings goes unwittingly to his doom, responds to the latter's announcement that he will stay for dinner at the Tower, with a confidential postscript:

And supper too, although thou knowst it not. (3, 3, 119–20)

But the chief equivocator is, of course, Richard himself, who identifies his characteristic manipulation of language:

> Thus, like the formal Vice Iniquity,
> I moralize two meanings in one word.
>
> (3, 1, 82–83)

Richard's criminal actions in the play are almost always attended either by his own laughter or by laughter-provoking wit directed to the audience. Early in the play, for example, after he bids farewell to the doomed Clarence, he announces with mock seriousness: "I do love thee so / That I will shortly send thy soul to Heaven." As he explains to the audience,

> Why, I can smile, and murder whiles I smile,
> And cry "Content" to that which grieves my heart,
> And wet my cheeks with artificial tears,
> And frame my face to all occasions.
>
> (*Henry VI,* pt. 3, 3, 2, 182–85)

By way of demonstration, he jauntily attends to the burial of a victim: "first, I'll turn yon fellow in his grave."

More comic in words than in deeds, Richard exhibits a repertoire of diabolic wit that includes most of the traditional devices of wordplay associated with agents of evil. When he receives his mother's blessing, he reverses sacred language with a perverse acknowledgment:

> Amen, and make me die a good old man!
> That is the butt-end of a mother's blessing.
>
> (2, 2, 109–10)

He revises an ominous aside with innocent, similar-sounding words. Speaking with his nephew Prince Edward, he mutters, "So wise so young, they say do ne'er live long." When the boy asks him to repeat the remark, which he did not hear, the uncle promptly responds mendaciously, "I say, without characters fame lives long."

Along with verbal humor, one of the conventionally comic techniques of criminality is the disguise. Richard, who rings virtually every variation possible in his role as archvillain, also adopts a disguise. At a crucial moment in the action of the play, he appears before the mayor and citizens in a religious pose, with a prayerbook in his hand and with a bishop at each side. He pretends to be preoccupied in religious meditation, and when he is asked to accept the crown, he duly pleads reluctance to burden himself with a secular title. His refusal is properly equivocal, however: "I am unfit for state and majesty." This characteristically "truthful lie" is followed by his assumed outrage over Buckingham's profane oath, "Zounds!" He righteously protests, "O, do not swear, my lord of Buckingham." The crowning of hunchbacked Richard, histrionic as he is hypocritical, is the triumph of smiling evil.

Although not so centrally featured as in the portrayal of Richard, the techniques of comic criminality also provide a substratum of humor in the portrayal of Iago in *Othello*. The mood of jocularity is an important feature of this cynical villain. In his first appearance, as he defiles the quiet Venetian night by shouting obscenities below Brabantio's window, his language is designed to amuse as well as shock. A coarse humor lards his accusations: he warns Brabantio that "you'll have your daughter covered with a Barbary horse, you'll have your nephews neigh to you, you'll have coursers for cousins, and jennets for germans." In his subsequent conversations with his dupe Roderigo, his cynical vehemence rings comically in counterpoint to the absurd lamentations of this lovesick gull. In response to Roderigo's threatened suicide, he protests: "Ere I would say I would drown myself for the love of a guinea hen, I would change my humanity with a baboon." And by way of reply to Roderigo's worshipful praise of Desdemona, he retorts "Blest fig's end! The wine she drinks is made of grapes." His is the humor of the bluff, bluntly spoken cynic whose license with language ironically seems to confirm his honesty.

When Iago persuades Cassio to drink too much, humor is joined with conviviality, as Iago leads his fellow soldiers in singing. Spinning his web of evil to entrap Cassio as well as Othello and Desdemona, this "demi-devil" waves his wine glass with horrifying glee and sings: "And let me the cannikin clink, clink, / And let me the cannikin clink. A soldier's a man, / A life's but a span. Why, then let a soldier drink." At the end of the scene, Iago tosses a flippant question to the audience: "And what's he then that says I play the villain?" Throughout the play, his frank revelations to the audience often have the quality of sardonic gaiety. His criminality is for him a sport. His artful techniques are matters of gloating pride, and his boasts about them are almost always mirthful. He exerts himself, as he says, "but for my sport and profit," and his enjoyment is its own reward:

> . . . By the mass, 'tis morning!
> Pleasure and action make the hours seem short.
>
> (2, 3, 378–79)

Appalled by the depth and extent of their villainy, the reader is always surprised to realize that Richard III and Iago are also comic. Quite different is the case of the comic crew who are introduced in the company of Falstaff in the *Henry IV* plays and meet their appropriate fates as criminals during the action of *Henry V*. Here the reader laughs first, only to discover that full awareness of their villainy comes as somewhat of a surprise. The readers' gradual realization is essentially the same as that explained by the boy who serves the group but who decides that he must abandon them on moral principle despite his pleasure in their lively company. Although the speech is long, it is worth quoting in its entirety for its explicitness in correlating comic and criminal "antics":

> As young as I am, I have observed these three swashers. I am boy to them all three; but all they three, though they would serve me, could not be a man to me; for indeed three such antics do not amount to a man. For Bardolph, he is white-livered and red-faced; by the means whereof 'a faces it out, but fights not. For Pistol, he hath a killing tongue and a quiet sword; by the means whereof 'a breaks words, and keeps whole weapons. For Nym, he hath heard that men of few words are the best men, and therefore he scorns to say his prayers, lest 'a should be thought a coward; but his few bad words are matched with as few good deeds, for 'a never broke any man's head but his own, and that was against a post when he was drunk. They will steal any thing, and call it purchase. Bardolph stole a lute-case, bore it twelve leagues, and sold it for three half-pence. Nym and Bardolph are sworn brothers in filching; and in Calais they stole a fire-shovel. I knew by that piece of service the men would carry coals. They would have me as familiar with men's pockets as their gloves or their handkerchers; which makes much against my manhood, if I should take from another's pocket to put into mine; for it is plain pocketing up of wrongs. I must leave them, and seek some better service. Their villainy goes against my weak stomach, and therefore I must cast it up. (3, 2, 28–55)

Each of the three receives harsh punishment in the course of the action. Pistol, whose boastful cowardice recalls Falstaff, has been deceptive in claiming a soldier's career, and of him Captain Gower says:

> Why, 'tis a gull, a fool, a rogue, that now and then goes

> to the wars, to grace himself at his return into London under the form of a soldier. And such fellows are perfect in the great commanders' names, and they will learn you by rote where services were done; at such and such a sconce, at such a breach, at such a convoy; who came off bravely, who was shot, who disgraced, what terms the enemy stood on; and this they con perfectly in the phrase of war, which they trick up with new-tuned oaths. (3, 6, 69–79)

But he meets his punishment at the hands of a real soldier, Fluellen, who cudgels him into eating the Welsh leeks that he has so scorned! The punishment is not entirely a facetious one, however, for Pistol can contemplate for his future only a career as bawd when he returns to England.

Pistol's fellow thieves, Nym and Bardolph, are more severely punished. Bardolph's red nose, the subject of much mirth in the preceding play, is, as Fluellen says, "executed" and "his fire's out." We learn of the deaths of these rogues from their boy, who compares them with Pistol in terms of the devil and the Vice from his own playgoing experience.

> Bardolph and Nym had ten times more valour than this roaring devil i' th' old play, that everyone may pare his nails with a wooden dagger; and they are both hanged. (4, 4, 72–76)

Although Falstaff is spared death by hanging, he cannot be entirely dissociated from his henchmen who, unlike him, live long enough to follow the wars to France, only to die disgraced on foreign soil. But Falstaff is a multidimensional figure, who participates in several kinds of comic evil, of which his criminality is on the whole less important than his moral negation and his sensuality.

3

In some of Shakespeare's plays the comedy of evil focuses

on sensuality: the humor of the flesh, especially the sins of lust and gluttony. In these plays, where the animal nature of man is subjected to mockery, a symbolic setting of taverns and brothels is often provided as an arena for wanton appetites. As in the morality tradition, tavern merriment is rarely morally neutral; typically the amiable company and gay songs are instruments of devilish seduction. In particular the seductive appeal of tavern life was a standard feature of the Prodigal plays, which aimed at demonstrating those sins besetting youth.[8] In plays like *Nice Wanton* and *The Longer Thou Livest,* the youthful protagonists yield to the apparently innocent lure of mirth and music, only to fall more deeply into the serious practices of drinking, wenching, and gambling, and from there into lives of crime. *Nice Wanton* is typical in depicting this progressive moral deterioration but exceptional among the moralities for its tragic conclusion. Both of the deliquent children meet bad ends, with Ishmael hanged for crime and Delilah dead of the pox. Both travel to their doom on the primrose path of tavern conviviality. And in *The Longer Thou Livest,* the foolish protagonist Moros calls for a drink of wine on his deathbed, and Confusion carries him off to the "eternal fyre."

Shakespeare enters this marginal moral world of sensual vices in both *Measure for Measure* and *Henry IV, 1* and *2.* In the *Henry IV* plays, which participate directly in the homiletic structure of the Prodigal moralities, the tavern world is at the center of the action, with Prince Hal, the prodigal son, divided between the forces of the good, which are represented by his father, the Chief Justice, and others, and the forces of evil, which are represented by the world of Eastcheap and concentrated in the quintessential tavern tempter, Falstaff. In *Measure for Measure,* on the other hand, the world of taverns and "stews" remains in the background, a concretization of the moral decadence of Vienna, which the austere Angelo hopes to correct by his stern execution of the rigorous laws. Although both are at once funny and evil, these tavern worlds function differently in their respective plays.

In *Measure for Measure* the underworld of bawds and brothels is of major thematic importance, not merely establishing the decadent atmosphere of Vienna but also providing counterpoint to the sexual offense for which Claudio is sentenced to die. In direct contrast to the plighted troth and genuine love that unite Claudio and Julietta, is the profane and ugly, but amusing, professionalism of the stews, populated by such marginal citizens as Pompey the bawd and Mistress Overdone. As a businesswoman in vice, Mistress Overdone is dismayed when she learns of the new edict against her "hothouse": "Thus, what with the war, what with the sweat, what with the gallows, and what with poverty, I am custom-shrunk." But Pompey is cheerfully optimistic, sustained by his resourcefulness and his perverse faith in the worst of human nature. He recognizes that to outlaw brothels is "to geld and splay all the youth of the city," and on this conviction he can assure his mistress that she will always find customers.

When the stringent laws are enforced, however, Pompey is driven to seek a new trade. What he chooses to become is a hangman's assistant. But the transition from a bawd's to a hangman's helper is not so drastic as it may seem; it is merely a shift from "dying" to dying. And in prison he finds himself among old friends:

> I am as well acquainted here as I was in our house of profession: one would think it were Mistress Overdone's own house, for here be many of her old customers. First, here's young Master Rash; he's in for a commodity of brown paper and old ginger, ninescore and seventeen pounds, of which he made five marks, ready money: marry, then, ginger was not much in request, for the old women were all dead. Then is there here one Master Caper, at

> the suit of Master Three-Pile the mercer, for some four suits of peach-coloured satin, which now peaches him a beggar. Then have we here young Dizzy, and young Master Deep-Vow, and Master Copper-spur, and Master Starve-lackey, the rapier and daggerman, and young Drop-heir that killed lusty Pudding, and Master Forthright the tilter, and brave Master Shoe-tie the great traveler, and wild Halfcan that stabbed Pots, and, I think, forty more; all great doers in our trade, and are now "for the Lord's sake." (4, 3, 1–20)

An amusing but highly didactic roster! But Pompey will probably remain intransigent for, as he remarked to Escalus, who had advised him to change his way of life:

> I thank your worship for your good counsel; [aside] but I shall follow it as the flesh and fortune shall better determine. (2, 1, 252–54)

Most of the young men in this play follow good counsel only as "the flesh and fortune" determine. Along with the protagonist, Claudio, who is awaiting his doom for sins of the flesh, is the "fantastic," Lucio, who mediates between the seamy underworld and the ducal palace. Lucio is an ambivalent character, on the one hand an educated and aristocratic friend of the young gentleman Claudio, and on the other an intimate of such unsavory specimens as Overdone and Pompey. Lucio is an analogue to Claudio in that he, too, has got a young maid with child, but his punishment is marriage rather than death. From his point of view, however, marriage is the worse fate. "Marrying a punk, my lord, is pressing to death, whipping, and hanging." But ultimately his devotion to the flesh proves less dangerous than his propensity for slander, a crime for which he is—albeit temporarily—sentenced to death by hanging.

Lucio's multiple roles in the play are not all involved in the comedy of evil. In his role as friend and adviser to Isabella, Claudio's sister, he is neither evil nor funny. When he reports Claudio's imprisonment to the virtuous maiden, his language is respectful and decorous, and when he accompanies her during her first interview with Angelo, he acts as a cheering section to spur her on in her plea for mercy. When he appears in the company of Pompey, however, he changes his language from blank verse to prose and his role from sympathetic confidant of a nobleman to intimate pal of pimps and punks. When he is thus identified with the morally depraved world of Vienna, he becomes a comic exemplar of the sensual vices. He overreaches himself when he irreverently suggests that the Duke himself is but a lecher, one who would never enforce a sentence against fornication, his own favorite pastime.

Like the Vice, Lucio tries to slip away unnoticed when he is caught in the act, but the Duke recalls him and demands that he be punished for his shameless sensuality and heedless slander. An aristocrat, Lucio stands at one end of the social spectrum of vice in the play, with the illiterate "employees" of Mistress Overdone at the other, and an implied middle range is crowded with gallants like Drop-Heir and Master Rash. As in the moralities, moral condemnation and social satire meet.

Whereas in *Measure for Measure* the sensual vices of gluttony, sloth, and lechery are dispersed among several characters, as in a crowded Breughel canvas, in the *Henry IV* plays they are largely concentrated in one impressive figure of gigantic bulk, Falstaff. This epitome of the "fairer than honest" bon vivant fulfills the combined roles of a century of personifications of these separate vices. The prototype occurs in Henry Medwall's *Nature,* written about 1490, where his name is Gluttony and his pseudonym Good Fellowship.[9] As the other vices in the play assemble for battle against the forces of virtue, Gluttony appears on stage "with a cheese and a bottle," weapons that he considers superior to military arms:

What the devil harness should I miss,
Without it be a bottle?
Another bottle I will go purvey
Lest that drink be scarce in the way
Or happily none to sell.

(pt. 2, ll. 778–82)

Similarly, in John Rastell's *Nature of the Four Elements* (ca. 1517), the Vice called Sensual Appetite describes a "shrewd fray" in which he has been fighting in his own military fashion, boasting equivocally,

Yea, I have slain them every man,
Save them that ran away.

(p. 37)

Sensual Appetite, who lures his youthful victim to the pleasures of brothel and tavern even as Falstaff attracts the malingering Prince from his royal duties, also boasts with fanciful exaggeration of his prowess on the battlefield, in a way that distinctly anticipates the braggart of Eastcheap.

The roll call of Falstaff's ancestors could go on. But that Falstaff himself plays the role of seductive Vice is clear from the Prince's language (pt. 1):

that reverend vice, that grey iniquity, that father ruffian, that vanity in years. (2, 4, 453–54)

Appealing and amusing though he is—and the appeal and the amusement are essential by definition—Falstaff is evil insofar as he incarnates sensuality himself and as he distracts the young prince from the affairs of state and seduces him into a life of ease and pleasure rather than statesmanship and battle. His banishment is dramatically essential at the moment when Henry becomes king, but it is morally essential by definition, from the moment when we first encounter this "Good Fellowship" in the tavern at Eastcheap.

In his alehouse existence, Falstaff turns night into day, perverting time as he perverts the nature of man by surrendering reason to appetite. The Prince mockingly asks him:

> What a devil hast thou to do with the time of the day? unless hours were cups of sack, and minutes capons, and clocks the tongues of bawds, and dials the signs of leaping houses, and the blessed sun himself a fair hot wench in flame-colored taffeta, I see no reason why thou shouldst be so superfluous to demand the time of the day. (1, 2, 6–12)

The Prince's question leads in turn to his ominous prognosis of a life of evil which, as always, seems attractive at the present moment but quite overlooks temporal consequences. Falstaff pleads that he is content if the purse he snatches on Monday night can be but dissolutely spent on Tuesday morning.

Not in spite of but because of his wit, his ingratiating personality, his great story of the eleven men in buckram, his self-mockery as he puffingly climbs up steep Gadshill, his racy language, and his endless inventiveness, is lovable Sir John a danger, a "white-bearded Satan." Ironically, the Prince knows and tells:

> there is a devil haunts thee in the likeness of an old fat man; a tun of man is thy companion. Why dost thou converse with that trunk of humours, that bolting-hutch of beastliness, that swoll'n parcel of dropsies, that huge bombard of sack, that stuffed cloak bag o' guts, that roasted Manningtree ox with the pudding in his belly, that reverend vice, that grey iniquity, that father ruffian, that vanity in years? Wherein is he good, but to taste sack and drink it? Wherein neat and cleanly, but to carve a capon and eat it? Wherein cunning, but in craft? Wherein

crafty, but in villainy? Wherein villainous, but in all things? Wherein worthy, but in nothing? (2, 4, 446–59)

It is the audience, not the prince, who resists the lesson. As George Orwell once noted, we love Falstaff because he is evil, because he represents and objectifies the "Saturday self"—the "voice of the belly protesting against the soul. He it is who punctures your fine attitudes and urges you to look after Number One, to be unfaithful to your wife, to bilk your debts." The comedy of evil, though a stage convention based on Christian theology, is also a psychological fact.

But the Middle Ages and the Renaissance never quite forgot that one day the voice of the belly would be silenced and the soul would speak alone. For the Christian mind it was an easy transition from smiling sensuality to the gaping grin of antic death. A bizarre custom offers a striking case in point from the fifteenth century. In the crowded burial lot of the Church of the Innocents in Paris, amidst the piles of unburied bones, prostitutes kept their booths, busily hawking the flesh that they belied in the death's-head that they wore as insignia of their trade. In the plays of Shakespeare, as in those of his contemporaries, the theme of *memento mori* gives comic reverberations in complementary mockery of sensual sin and certain death. As Falstaff says to Doll Tearsheet sitting on his lap, "Do not speak like a death's-head. Do not bid me remember my end." (*Henry IV*, pt. 2, 4, 2, 39–40).

In one classic situation, at once parodying and embodying the Dance of Death tradition, the condemned criminal refuses to die. In *Measure for Measure,* the stubborn criminal Barnardine refuses to submit to the death sentence, thereby adding his name to the long roster of morality figures of evil who similarly rejected death. Before Barnardine appears, we are informed that he is a prisoner of nine years' standing, "a man that apprehends death no more dreadfully, but as a drunken sleep; careless, reckless, and fearless of what's past, present, or to come; insensible of mortality, and desperately mortal." When Abhorson, the executioner, urges him one more time to come forth from his cell and face death, he growls from within, unwilling to move. Pompey tries polite persuasion: "You must be good, sir, to rise and be put to death." Barnardine then appears, but protests the warrant for execution on grounds that he has been drinking all night and is not fit for it. Even the consoling language of the Duke, disguised as a friar, makes no impression on this intransigent villain. Speaking in the tradition of Vices like Haphazard (*Appius and Virginia*) and Iniquity (*Nice Wanton*) and characters like Pedringano (*Spanish Tragedy*), he staunchly and simply refuses to die:

> I have been drinking hard all night, and I will have more time to prepare me, or they shall beat out my brains with billets. I will not consent to die this day, that's certain. . . . I swear I will not die today for any man's persuasion. (4, 3, 55–57, 60–61)

But death will come, beckoning with his bony hand. Although Barnardine is spared in the context of a comic ending in a particular play, the last laugh belongs to death, who awaits each and every mortal dancing partner. The leering figure of "antic death" is described with unusual poetic beauty in *Richard II,* where it is linked with the body politic image, universalizing its implicatons:

> For God's sake let us sit upon the ground
> And tell sad stories of the death of kings:
> How some have been deposed, some slain in war,
> Some haunted by the ghosts they have deposed,
> Some poisoned by their wives, some sleeping killed,
> All murdered—for within the hollow crown
> That rounds the mortal temples of a king
> Keeps Death his court, and there the antic sits,

Scoffing his state and grinning at his pomp,
Allowing him a breath, a little scene,
To monarchize, be feared, and kill with looks.
Infusing him with self and vain conceit,
As if this flesh which walls about our life
Were brass impregnable; and, humored thus,
Comes at the last, and with a little pin
Bores thorough his castle wall, and farewell king!

(3, 2, 155–70)

The effect of the traditional image of a grinning personification of death is enriched here through its combination with the microcosmic image: antic death keeps his court within this little kingdom of man, vulnerable through its futile walls of flesh.

The comic treatment of the *memento mori* tradition again combines with the mockery of sensuality in the graveyard scene in *Hamlet*. Wise fools that the gravediggers are, they comment philosophically about death as they go about their grim work of digging a new grave. They engage in amusing quibbles over the technicalities of suicide, questioning whether the corpse they are about to bury was drowned "wittingly" or "unwittingly." Then they undertake a series of humorous riddles, all with answers involving death, thus investing their morbid occupation with comic detachment. One clown asks who it is that builds stronger than a mason, a shipwright, or a carpenter, and the other promptly responds that it is the gallowsmaker, "for that frame outlives a thousand tenants." But the clown is not satisfied with this answer to his riddle, for he knows one that touches more closely upon his profession. Impatiently he explains:

Cudgel thy brains no more about it, for your dull ass will not mend his pace with beating. And when you are asked this question next, say "a gravemaker." The houses he makes lasts till doomsday. (5, 1, 57–60)

And the cheerful diggers continue their labors with song. But even the song is a wry comment on the inevitability of death:

> But age with his stealing steps
> Hath clawed me in his clutch,
> And hath shipped me into the land,
> As if I have never been such.
>
> (5, 1, 72–75)

But the scene takes a different didactic turn when Hamlet identifies the skull of Yorick the jester, whom he knew as a boy. In a series of ironic questions addressed to the skull, he meditates the two-way comedy of mortality. The gibes and mocks of Yorick the living jester are simply repeated by the grinning skull of Yorick the dead jester. Chap'fallen death himself is a jester. And to Hamlet's mind the mocking deaths-head offers another joke, this time about the delusion of sensuality. The skull becomes an image of frail woman-kind, vainly hiding from age and death under the veneer of cosmetics:

> Now get you to my lady's chamber, and tell her, let her paint an inch thick, to this favor she must come. Make her laugh at that. (5, 1, 194–97)

The mocking apparition of death even casts its shadow over that abundantly sensual jester Falstaff. From his first question to Prince Hal on the subject—"Shall there be gallows standing in England when thou art king?"—to the news of the death by hanging of his cronies Nym and Bardolph, the image of the gallows is an object of grim jocularity. Falstaff objects that Mistress Doll Tearsheet talks like a death's-head, and Bardolph appears to him as a veritable penitential picture: "I never see thy face but I think upon hellfire" (3, 3, 32). Throughout the two-part play, in the background of merriment and ribaldry, there gapes the grave thrice wider for Falstaff than for other men. For Shakespeare, then, bestial behavior and physical death are both subject to the mordant mockery that implies their temporality and insubstantiality.

4

Although the Falstaff of *Henry IV* Part 1 is primarily a figure of sensuality, an embodiment of appetite, the Falstaff who reappears in Part 2 only to be banished by the king is, as a recent editor notes, "the walking embodiment of everything the play rejects."[10] Many of Shakespeare's plays include such a character, or group of characters, who represent the repudiation of all the positive values asserted in the world of the play. These figures offer still another dimension of the comedy of evil, the "moral negative." Whether or not these moral negatives are criminals or sensualists, the demonstration of their moral negation is contrapuntally comic. In the typically Shakespearean dramatic structure, which provides a continuum of comment on a central idea through a variety of encompassing characters and actions, the *homo repudiandus* occupies the negative pole, a comic position by definition.

Falstaff is more complex as a moral negative than as an embodiment of appetite. He negates several values important both to the king and the country: health, order, courage, honesty, honor, and justice. In Part 2, where he becomes more of a monologist than a conversationalist, he even repudiates the conviviality that made him so attractive in Part 1. His negation of honesty through both theft and dissimulation, which was introduced in the Gadshill robbery scenes in Part 1, is deepened in the sequel, where the defiance of law has serious consequences and where boyish pranks undergo a solemn metamorphosis into adult crimes.

Early in the play an encounter between Falstaff and the Chief Justice establishes the moral lines of force within the play, since the dignified figure of authority personally stands for all the civilized values that fat Sir John rejects.[11] The Chief Justice identifies him as the prince's "ill angel," a charge that Falstaff naturally denies in his own equivocal way. His denial ends with a profession of youth, which the Chief Justice quickly counters with a vivid description of the old man's dry hand, yellow cheek, white beard, decreasing leg, increasing belly, double chin, broken voice, and every part "blasted with antiquity." Sir John also repudiates justice when he tries to escape Mistress Quickly's charges against him. He is more than reluctant to "pay the debt" and "unpay the villainy." And he manifestly negates justice in his bribery of recruits for the army.

Falstaff negates health through his continual references to disease and medicine. Much more than in Part 1, the old man is preoccupied with the ailments of age. He responds to the Chief Justice's bleak comments on his age with a cynical recognition:

> A man can no more separate age and covetousness than 'a can part young limbs and lechery. But the gout galls the one and the pox pinches the other, and so both the degrees prevent my curses. (1, 2, 239–42)

Not that the recognition changes his way of life:

> A good wit will make use of anything. I will turn diseases to commodity. (1, 2, 258–9)

Even his disquisition on the uses of sherris-sack is prompted by the fact of disease, for he propounds the use of drink as a panacea. But at least Sir John cries out against sack on his deathbed—or so we are told in the amusingly touching scene in *Henry V*—avoiding the final folly of his ancestor

Moros, who called for another drink in his last moments.

The tragedy of *Romeo and Juliet* offers another moral negative in the ingratiating person of Mercutio. This play contains a spectrum of attitudes toward love, ranging from the idealization of love, which proves fatal to the young protagonists, to the smutty jocularity of the servants. In the larger, background world of the play, the city of Verona, the love theme assumes the form of civility, with the Prince's final reconciliation of the feuding houses of Capulet and Montague putting an end to the hatred and civil dissension that have rent the community and turned citizens against fellow citizens.

Paralleling the Prince as a symbol of harmony is the Friar, representing the church, who makes a well-meaning but fatal attempt to preserve the sacramental value of married love in his young friends. Falling far short of the transcendental values represented by these two symbolic figures are the two sets of parents, themselves apparently exemplars of loveless, arranged marriages, and blindly dedicated to social success rather than personal happiness. Still further below the ideal are the earthly attitudes so volubly expressed by Juliet's aging nurse, whose sentimental reminiscences are tinged with bawdiness and whose loyalties respond readily to pragmatic pressures.

The Nurse's spontaneous responsiveness to Mercutio (2, 4) hints at a common denominator in their temperaments, and it is with these two figures that the projection of the love theme enters the negative side of the ledger. Like the nurse, Romeo's buoyant friend is an attractive character, and his association with evil is only in terms of his position in respect to the one absolute value, love. For in his cynical disparagement of romantic love he is not merely a foil to Romeo, but also the privative—and comic—side of that positive value which unifies and informs the many elements of the play. His wit is obscene though sparkling—Shaw remarked amusingly that when Mercutio approached a woman, he himself would shiver with apprehension as to what vulgarity he would come out with. When he learns of Romeo's solitary walks at dawn, Mercutio denigrates such sentimentality with bawdy banter:

> Now will he sit under a medlar tree
> And wish his mistress were that kind of fruit
> As maids call medlars when they laugh alone.
>
> (2, 1, 34–36)

Ultimately he even jests himself to death: "Ask for me tomorrow and you will find me a grave man" (3, 1, 98–100).

But Mercutio manifests only one dimension of comic evil, namely, the mocking negation—albeit witty and innocently verbal—of an ideal. In some of Shakespeare's comedies dealing with the subject of love, however, the negative attitude is embodied in grim rather than gay figures for the purpose of dramaturgic contrast. In both cases, the threats posed by the would-be villains are proved insubstantial. Neither the bold laughter of Mercutio nor the sour countenances of such ominous images of negation as vulturous Shylock, ill-willed Malvolio, and melancholy Don John are permitted to stifle the values upheld by the protagonists of the plays. The ultimate defeat of the morally negative figures effectively vindicates the values that they denied.

Whether the role of Shylock is actually funny or whether its comic counterpoint is beyond laughter is a moot question, since he is a particularly sympathetic character for modern audiences, who are sensitive to racial and religious intolerance in ways that the Elizabethans were not. But although a strand of affective sentiment is woven into the character of Shylock, permitting him on a universal level to symbolize victims of such intolerance, it should not obscure the equally palpable strand of absurdly comic perversion. Shylock as an individual, not simply as a member of a despised minority, reverses the value of Christian charity that informs the action of the play, and even behaves so abominably in his own home that his daughter dreads his presence and is ready to elope, and his servant deserts him as a very devil of an employer. Surely the scene in which he passionately equates his daughter and his ducats is intended to be funny, and certainly his behavior at the trial, as he hails the youthful, unknown lawyer as a second Daniel come to offer judgment, is funny as well as ironic. Even his deflated departure from the scene of the trial, if not totally biased by an actor determined to make Shylock a tragic hero, is laughable, as he weakly excuses himself by saying "I am not well."

Somewhat analogous to Shylock in his puritanical negation of gaiety and romance is Malvolio, the sullen steward in *Twelfth Night.* Like Shylock, he too is the inevitable victim of a witty and wholesome society that cannot brook such a sober, uncivil member. Malvolio's nature—his nominal ill will—negates the standards postulated in the festive, generous, aristocratic world of Olivia's estate. He rejects not merely love and friendship but even conviviality. He is a social climber, an egoist, a vain man too absurdly in love with himself to recognize his smug face as it appears to his companions. The climax of his comic embarrassment occurs in the scene with the clown, disguised as curate in order to torment and confuse the imprisoned steward. The clown plays the role with infernal glee, comparing his assumed role with that of the "old Vice" with his "dagger of lath." To behold such grim faces as those of Shylock and Malvolio gives one heartburn, as Beatrice so aptly remarks of Don John in *Much Ado.* And although not all of the figures of moral negation in Shakespeare's plays are actually villainous —Mercutio, for example, who is a walking repudiation of idealism in love but by no means a villain—they do participate in the privative realm of evil, even when in a comic context they may appear appealing through their wit and humor, or sympathetic through their isolation from the comic world about them.

When the moral negative is also a villainous figure, however, it is important to note that the comic demonstration of his negation is primarily thematic and often quite unrelated to his comic techniques conventionally employed in the performance of evil deeds. Iago, for example, embodies comic evil in two entirely different ways. On the one hand, as a villain, he is comic in his mirthful, diabolic plotting against Othello. On the other, he is also comic in his jaunty negation of ideal love and marital fidelity. When he first arrives in Cyprus, he engages in bawdy jocularity with Desdemona and Emilia on the subject of women. He mocks them for their sensuality and deprecates their role in marriage:

. . . you are pictures out of door;
Bells in your parlours, wildcats in your kitchens,
Saints in your injuries, devils being offended,
Players in your housewifery, and housewives in your beds.

(2, 1, 108–11)

Over Desdemona's demurring response, he exclaims:

Nay, it is true, or else I am a Turk:
You rise to play, and go to bed to work.

(2, 1, 112–13)

Dissociated from his villainy, such cynical remarks remind us of the bawdy jocularity of Mercutio, whose disparaging attitudes toward love and marriage are similarly expressed. Certainly they in no way necessitated villainous action. As comic *homo repudiandus* Iago is essentially a satirist, summing up his condemnation of womankind with a withering definition of their role: "to suckle fools and chronicle small beer." In this dimension of his role in the play, Iago is like a witty forerunner of Goethe's Mephistopheles, "the spirit that denies."

Two of Shakespeare's late romances also contain particularly interesting examples of the comic moral negative. In the same tradition, they are different only insofar as the world of the romances is different. In these late plays, which have occasioned much commentary in recent years, certain recurring themes assume particular prominence: the conflict of nature and art, the significance of education, the importance of courtesy and civility, the value of forgiveness, the possibility of regeneration. Throughout Shakespeare's career civilization is a supreme "good," and evil is continually associated with the barbaric. In the climactic romances, "civility" is the focus of virtue. As Imogen puts it in *Cymbeline,* "breach of custom is breach of all." Consequently the evil in these plays involves breach of custom, of civility, of courtesy and harmonious behavior. The comedy of evil—in *The Tempest* and *Cymbeline*—is concentrated on a boorish, uncivilized individual, incapable of education, a lout on whom human nature chafes like an ill-fitting garment.

Granville-Barker first noticed the strong resemblance between Caliban and Cloten, calling the latter "a civilized Caliban." Certainly many parallels exist between these two figures, both products of civilization without being genuinely civilized. Both play negative roles, opposing the values of their particular societies. Both are boorish in a world that treasures civility, both lustful in a world that puts a high moral and poetic premium on chastity, both with delusions of grandeur about conquering those worlds in which their very presence is so alien. More specifically—and more complexly—"headless" Cloten and "fishy" Caliban are effective symbolic negations in the important theme of the relationship between art and nature, and between nurture and nature.

First, a closer look at Cloten. He first appears after he has obviously made a foolish spectacle of himself in a duel. His own conceit blinds him to his own cowardice and lack of skill while the first Lord hypocritically consoles his wounded vanity. Between the ridiculous boasts of the braggart, however, the second Lord keeps the audience informed through a series of mocking asides. Essentially the same scene is repeated later in the first act, after Cloten has lost at bowls. Again the two accompanying lords offer an antiphonal response with the egregious flattery of the one weighed against the delightfully mocking commentary of the other. Cloten tops off the conversation with a hilariously ironic statement that places him squarely in the long line of equivocating vices:

> I had rather not be so noble as I am. (2, 1, 19)

In the second act Cloten clumsily pursues his sexual ambitions. Chastity is a central theme in *Cymbeline,* and the fidelity of Imogen to her deceived husband is exalted as a virtue. Cloten, on the other hand, is primitive and brutal in his appetites—like his savage counterpart Caliban—and muses happily on the fanciful scene of his intended rape of Imogen in the presence of her husband's corpse. Unlike Caliban, however, he is lacking in sensitivity to music (one of the few advantages of savagery over depraved civilization) and hires musicians to serenade (and "penetrate") the pure Imogen. His crude lapse into bawdy double meaning is in sharp contrast both to the chaste object of his base intentions and to the charming lyric offered on the occasion. His indifference to music recalls, by the way, an earlier and quite different comic villain, who closed the windows of his house to keep out the festive strains of music in commercial Venice.

Eventually Cloten's stupidity and rudeness strain the patience of even Imogen, however, and when he has the foolish temerity to call her husband "base," she exclaims that she would prefer Posthumous's "meanest garment" to the very person of Cloten. Imogen's remark tortures the dull wits of Cloten, and he broods over the insult. After killing Posthumous, he decides, he will rape Imogen while dressed in the dead man's clothes. The symbolism of garments and accoutrements, a traditional vehicle for the themes of nobility and the conflict of nature and nurture, comes to focus on Cloten, with an ambivalence of serious and comic implications that climaxes in his death scene. Before he meets his fitting symbolic demise, however, Cloten establishes his negative role in still another thematic facet of the play. Together with his mother, the wicked queen, he opposes the payment of British tribute to the Roman emperor, Caesar Augustus. The value scheme of the play obviously favors the tribute to Augustus: the Roman virtues are necessary to the civilizing of ancient Britain; Jupiter, the presiding Roman deity, appears in the dream that climaxes the play; all the Romans are portrayed as admirable; and, after harmony has been restored at the end of the play, Cymbeline agrees to pay the tribute even though he has defeated the Romans in battle.[12]

But the climax of Cloten's derisive career occurs in the pastoral setting of part of the play, which, by his very presence as well as by his bestial and violent actions, he violates. Dressed in the appropriated garments of Posthumous, Cloten sets out to destroy the innocence of Imogen and is instead destroyed by the innocence of her brother, Guiderius. Cloten challenges the young prince, who is unaware of his own royal lineage that nonetheless reveals itself in his very word and gesture. Ironically, the stupid Cloten, on whom "nurture" would stick scarcely more than on Caliban, insultingly calls Guiderius a "slave," a "mountaineer." In spite of his royal blood—for Cloten is a prince, as Belarius dutifully reminds us—his nature lacks the seed that can be nurtured by education. In contrast, Guiderius, because of his royal blood and blessed with the seed that can benefit from nurture, reveals his nobility even in the confines of a cave and the wilds of primitive life far from courtly training.

Cloten's death, then, is highly symbolic, the physical loss merely substantiating the intellectual and spiritual emptiness. He dies literally (as did Macbeth metaphorically) in borrowed garments, so that his beheading leaves him without identity. Guiderius's wry comment on the detached head is at least metaphysically funny: it is an "empty purse."

Like *Cymbeline, The Tempest* is concerned with the theme of education. As Frank Kermode has pointed out, carefully drawn parallels between the education of Miranda and that of Caliban are established at the beginning of the play and developed throughout the subsequent action.[13] Miranda's education in isolation has been highly effective: with the help of Prospero's library her innate, aristocratic capacity for learning has been nurtured and fulfilled. In contrast, Caliban's education simply did not take. As he bitterly puts it, as a result of being taught language, he has learned only to curse. Caliban by his very nature—"a savage and deformed slave"—is incapable of absorbing genuine education, and the play demonstrates the futility of Prospero's well-meaning attempt to provide him with one. This monstrous offspring of a devil and a witch will never be capable of the education that brings order and harmony out of chaos and confusion, civilization out of barbarism. He will remain on his lonely island, a "thing of darkness."

Since in the world of *The Tempest* proper education is a "good," it follows that either the lack or the corruption of education is evil. Caliban's comic role thus coincides with his role as the moral negation of education and all that it implies for human civilization. He inevitably opposes the important Renaissance principle of hierarchy. In his first meeting with the drunken Stephano and Trinculo, he advances his plan for seizing the island out of his master's grasp. In what is unquestionably one of the funniest scenes in the play, the three unregenerates—one savage and two corrupted products of civilization—plan a conspiracy to take control of the island. Caliban's imaginative violence suggests multiple means of killing Prospero, but in his limited and literal mentality, he stresses the destruction of Prospero's books.To him the books are magically endowed physical objects; he seems incapable of understanding that knowledge can be abstracted from the printed page.

Along with this anarchic intention to overthrow Prospero —which is rendered doubly funny through the sudden debility of his fellow anarchists—Caliban voices his lustful ambition to possess Miranda. Just as Miranda's sophisticated education is contrasted with Caliban's brute ignorance, so her innocence and purity are contrasted with his wholly bestial appetites. We learn very early in the play that Prospero had let Caliban share his cell until the latter threatened Miranda's chastity. Lacking in civilized restraints, Caliban is a monstrous threat, but comic in his bungling attempts to carry out his intended rape. He is also in this connection sharply contrasted with Ferdinand, who assures Prospero that his sense of honor is quite capable of subduing his "liver," so that Miranda's premarital chastity is in no danger whatsoever.

Just as his sexual desires are uncontrollable, so Caliban finds intemperate pleasure in alcohol. One taste from Stephano's bottle convinces him that this man must be a god to possess such an elixir, and another comic highlight of the play follows when the intoxicated Caliban bursts into stammering song: "Ban-ban-c-c-Caliban, get a new master, get a new man."

When Caliban appears in Act 4 (his appearances occur symmetrically, one in each act) , he and his companions have been subjected to the sobering influence of a dip in a horse pond. But although the three conspirators are equally "all wet," the scene points up a contrast between the corrupt civilized vice and the primitive "natural" vice. Caliban's elemental thoughts are focused on the rape of Miranda and the murder of his hated master. Stephano and Trinculo, on the other hand, are diverted from their political ambitions by the sight of frippery on a clothes line.

In the resolution of the action in Act 5, the emphasis, as in all four of the late romances, is on harmony, forgiveness, and regeneration. Restoration of order does not involve punishment, as in the tragedies, or expulsion, as in the comedies. Instead, human nature is transposed, so to speak, into a higher key of civilized behavior. This is not to say that total or universal regeneration is possible, although perhaps the possibility of regeneration is, like the fact of the Fall, a necessary part of the definition of being human. It is significant that Caliban is not really human, and that the disguised and headless body of Cloten seems more a travesty of human nature than a real corpse. In any case, it is clear that civilization must be purged of its base elements, and purgation can only follow the laughter of recognition. In the rarefied atmosphere of the romances, the comedy of evil functions to provide this laughter of recognition.

5

In summary, then, Shakespeare's concern with the subject of evil led him, as it did his contemporaries, to draw upon the venerable stage tradition of homiletic mockery. Inevitably, the particular form adopted for the mockery depended upon the particular aspect of evil to be mocked; hence the variety of comic evil, ranging from the tavern wit of Falstaff to the cynical jests of Iago, from the pompous antics of Malvolio to the crude foolery of Cloten. Awareness of this homiletic tradition can serve as a useful corrective in staging, for many a performance of *Othello* or of *Richard III* has been marred by an anachronistic notion of a serious, brooding villain.[14] But above all, a full recognition of Shakespeare's dramatization of the comedy of evil helps to clarify the moral meaning of many otherwise thematically puzzling scenes.

With this consideration of the plays of Shakespeare, my survey of the "gargoyle element" in the English early drama is complete. This study has traced the historical origin and the artistic application of an idea. Medieval Christianity formulated a definition of evil as negation, which in turn cultivated an attitude toward negative evil as philosophically comic. The manifestations of a theoretically funny evil appeared in medieval art and became established as a convention in medieval and Renaissance drama. The comedy of evil is an unbroken thematic and dramaturgic thread extending from the medieval mysteries and moralities through the transitional interludes to the Elizabethan-Jacobean tragedies and comedies. Ultimately, this view of evil as a subject for mocking laughter provides one of the most profound and significant continuities in the history of English drama, culminating in the superb stage images of Shakespeare.

Notes to Chapter 6

1. Records confirm that touring companies played in Stratford in the early 1570s. In all probability their repertory included largely moralities and histories with morality features. R. Willis, born the same year as Shakespeare, in *Mount Tabor: Or Private Exercises of a Penitent Sinner* (1639) recalled a performance of *The Cradle of Security* that he saw as a boy in the town of Gloucester. The description of the play establishes it as a morality.

2. This idea is developed more fully in my "Macbeth and Dante's Inferno," *North Dakota Quarterly* 28 (Spring 1960) : 50–52. See also Walter Clyde Curry, *Shakespeare's Philosophical Patterns* (Baton Rouge, La., 1937) , and G. R. Elliott, *Dramatic Providence in Macbeth* (Princeton, N.J., 1958) .
3. One of the best essays on the porter scene is still William de Quincy's "On Knocking at the Gate in Macbeth." Although he did not know the medieval dramatic tradition, de Quincy perceived the general signification with remarkable literary insight. Samuel Taylor Coleridge, on the other hand, contrary to his usual perceptivity about Shakespeare, regarded the scene as an unfortunate excrescence.
4. The porter's references to equivocation are sometimes interpreted topically as referring to the contemporary Jesuit controversy over the meaning of *equivocation.* The topical allusion seems to me much less relevant than the relationship of the scene to the Christian tradition, which had all along recognized the equivocal nature of evil. In any case, the former is subsumed in the latter.
5. Although there is no evidence that Shakespeare had any knowlledge of *The Divine Comedy,* the many precise analogues to the *Inferno* in *Macbeth* as so striking as to arouse speculation. See my "Macbeth and Dante's Inferno," 28: 50–52.
6. The elaborate pun on *lie* echoes the witches' lies "like truth."
7. See chaps. 3 and 4, passim. Cf. *Mankind,* 1. 447: Tyt. "I com with my legges under me!"
8. Actually, the first tavern scene on stage occurs in a biblical play, the Digby *Mary Magdalene,* in which the analagous figure is Lechery. But tavern scenes later become part of the formula of Prodigal Son morality plays. For a summary of tavern humor in the moralities, see Normand Berlin, *The Base String: The Underworld in Elizabethan Drama* (South Brunswick, N.J., 1968) .
9. The resemblance was first noted in Spivack, *Allegory of Evil,* q. v.
10. See Norman Holland's introduction to the Signet edition of *Henry IV,* Part 2, p. xxxix.
11. See Dover Wilson, *The Fortunes of Falstaff* (Cambridge, 1943) .
12. See D. B. C. Marsh, *The Recurring Miracle* (Lincoln, Neb., 1962) for a similar reading of the Roman theme.
13. *The Tempest* (Arden Shakespeare) , ed. Frank Kermode (London, 1954) .
14. In the 1970 performance, the Shakespeare Memorial Theatre production at Stratford emphasized the comic aspects of Richard's role, with great success.

Bibliography

Abelard, Peter. *Scito Teipsum.* Translated by J. R. McCallum. In *Abelard's Ethics.* Oxford, 1955.

Adams, Joseph Q. *Chief Pre-Shakespearean Dramas.* Cambridge, Mass., 1924.

Adolf, Helen. "On Medieval Laughter." *Speculum* 22 (April 1947) : 251–53.

Alighieri, Dante. *The Divine Comedy: Hell.* Translated by Dorothy Sayers. Harmondsworth, 1949.

———. "De Vulgari Eloquentia." Translated by A. G. Gerrers Howell. In *The Great Critics,* edited by James Smith and Edd Parks, pp. 133–44. New York, 1939.

Apius and Virginia. Edited by R. B. McKerrow. Malone Society Reprint. Oxford, 1911.

Aquinas, Thomas. *Basic Writings of Thomas Aquinas.* Edited by A. Pegis. 2 vols. New York, 1945.

Auden, W. H. "Music and Shakespeare." In *Shakespeare Criticism 1936–60,* edited by Ann Ridler, pp. 306–28. London, 1963.

Augustine. *Confessions.* Translated by R. S. Pine Coffiin. Baltimore, Md., 1961.

Bale, John. *Three Laws.* Edited by A. Schroerer, *Anglia* 5 (1882).

Benesch, Otto. *The Art of the Renaissance in Northern Europe.* rev. ed. Cambridge, Mass., 1965.

Berlin, Normand. *The Base String: The Underworld in Elizabethan Drama.* Rutherford, N.J., 1968.

Bevington, David. *From Mankind to Marlowe.* Cambridge, Mass., 1962.

Blickling Homilies, edited by R. Morris. London, 1880.

Boethius. *Consolation of Philosophy.* Translated by W. V. Cooper. London, 1902; reprint ed. 1940.

Bukofzer, Manfred. "Speculative Thinking in Medieval Music." *Speculum* 17 (April 1942) : 165–80.

Burch, George B. *Early Medieval Philosophy.* New York, 1951.

Carpenter, Nan. "Music in Doctor Faustus." *Notes and Queries* 195 (1950) : 180–81.

Cecil, Lord David. *Poets and Story Tellers.* Indianapolis, Ind., 1964.

Chambers, E. K. *The Elizabethan Stage.* 4 vols. Oxford, 1923.

———. *The Medieval Stage.* 2 vols. Oxford, 1903.

Chapman, George. *The Widow's Tears.* Edited by Ethel Smeak. Lincoln, Neb., 1966.

Chaucer, Geoffrey. *Troilus and Criseyde.* Edited by R. K. Root. Princeton, N.J., 1926.

Chester Plays. Pt. 1, edited by Hermann Deimling. Oxford, 1892; reprint ed., 1968. Pt. 2, edited by Dr. Matthews. Oxford, 1916; reprint ed., 1968.

Clyomon and Clamydes. Edited by W. W. Greg. Malone Society Reprint. Oxford, 1913.

Cohen, Gustav. Editor. *Mystères et moralités.* Paris, 1920.

———, ed. *Recueil de farces Françaises inédites de la XVe siècle.* Reprint ed., Cambridge, Mass., 1949.

Common Conditions. Edited by C. F. Tucker Brooke. Elizabethan Club Reprints. New Haven, Conn., 1915.

Craig, Hardin. "Morality Plays and Elizabethan Drama." *Shakespeare Quarterly* 1 (1950) : 64–72.

———. "The Paternoster Play." *Nation* 104 (1917) : 563–64.

Curry, Walter C. *Shakespeare's Philosophical Patterns.* Baton Rouge, La., 1937.

Daniels, Samuel. *Poems.* Edited by Arthur C. Sprague. Cambridge, Mass., 1939.

Dekker, Thomas. *The Dramatic Works of Thomas Dekker.* Edited by Fredson Bowers. 4 vols. Cambridge, 1953–61.

Dessen, Alan. "The Alchemist: Jonson's Estates Play." *Renaissance Drama* 7 (1964) : 35–54.

———. "Volpone and the Late Morality Tradition." *Modern Language Quarterly* 25 (1964) : 383–99.

Digby Plays. Edited by F. J. Furnivall. Oxford, 1896. Reprint ed., 1967.

Dionysius. *The Works of Dionysius the Aeropagite.* Translated by John Parker. London, 1897–99.

Dodsley Robert, ed. *A Select Collection of Old English Plays.* 4th ed., revised by W. C. Hazlitt. 15 vols. London, 1874–76.

Elliott, G. R. *Dramatic Providence in "Macbeth."* Princeton, N.J., 1958.

Everyman. Edited by John Sket. Louvain, 1909.

Farnham, Willard. "The Medieval Comic Spirit in the English Renaissance." In *Joseph Quincy Adams Memorial Studies,* pp. 429–38. Washington, 1948.

———. *The Medieval Heritage of Elizabethan Tragedy.* rev. ed. Berkeley, Calif., 1936.

Ford, John. *The Broken Heart.* Edited by Brian Morris. New York, 1965.

———. *'Tis Pity She's A Whore.* Edited by Brian Morris. New York, 1968.

———. *Dramatic Works.* Edited by W. Bang and Henry de Vocht. 2 vols. Louvain, 1908 and 1927.

Fournier, Edouard, ed. *Le Théâtre Français avant la Renaissance, 1450–1550: Mystères, moralités, et farces.* Paris, 1874.

Garter, Thomas. *Virtuous and Godly Susanna.* Malone Society Reprint. Oxford, 1937.

Gibbon, Charles. *Remedie of Reason.* London, 1589.

Guazzo, Francesco Marias. *Compendium Maleficorum.* Edited by Rev. Montague Summers. Translated by E. A. Ashwin. London, 1929.

Holbein, Hans. *The Dance of Death.* New York, 1947.

Jonson, Ben. *Ben Jonson.* Edited by C. H. Herford and Percy Simpson. 11 vols. Oxford 1925–52.

King Darius. Edited by Alois Brandl. In *Quellen des weltlichen*

Dramas in England vor Shakespeare. Strasbourg, 1898.

Kolve, V. A. *The Play Called Corpus Christi.* Stanford, Calif., 1966.

Krautheimer, Richard. "Iconography of Medieval Architecture." *Journal of the Warburg and Courtauld Institute* 5 (1942).

Kyd, Thomas. *The Spanish Tragedy.* Edited by Philip Edwards. London, 1959.

Lacroix, Paul, ed. *Recueil de farces, soties et moralités.* Paris, 1859.

Langland, William. *Piers Plowman.* Edited by W. W. Skeat. 2 vols. Oxford, 1886.

LeDuc, Viollet, ed. *Ancien Théâtre Français.* 3 vols. Paris, 1854.

Leff, Gordon. *Medieval Thought.* Harmondsworth, 1958.

Lewis, C. S. *Preface to Paradise Lost.* New York, 1942.

Lovejoy, Arthur O. *The Great Chain of Being.* Cambridge, Mass., 1936.

Ludus Coventriae. Edited by K. S. Block. Oxford, 1922. Reprint ed., 1960.

Lupton, Thomas. *All for Money.* Edited by Edgar Schell and J. D. Shuchter in *English Morality Plays and Moral Interludes.* New York, 1969.

Lydgate, John. *The Dance of Death.* Edited Florence Warren. Oxford, 1931.

Macro Plays. Edited by Mark Eccles. Oxford, 1969.

Male, Emile. *The Gothic Image.* Translated by Doris Nussey. New York, 1913; reprint ed., 1961.

Malone Society Collections. vols. 1–3. Oxford, 1909.

Manly, J. M. "Literary Forms and the New Theory of the Origin of Species." *Modern Philology* 4 (April 1907) : 577–95.

———. *Specimens of the Pre-Shakespearean Drama.* 2 vols. Boston, 1897.

Marichal, Robert, ed. *Le Théâtre en France au Moyen Age.* Paris, 1909.

Marlowe, Christopher. *Works.* Edited by C. F. Tucker-Brooke. Oxford, 1910.

Marsh, D. B. C. *The Recurring Miracle.* Lincoln, Neb., 1962.

Marriage between Wit and Wisdom. Francis Merbury? Edited by J. O. Halliwell. Shakespeare Society, vol. 31. London, 1846.

Marston, John. *The Dutch Courtesan*. Edited by M. L. Wine. Lincoln, Neb., 1965.

———. *The Malcontent*. Edited by M. L. Wine. Lincoln, Neb., 1964.

Materialien zur Kunde des älteren englischen Dramas. Edited by W. Bang. Continued as *Materials for the study of old English drama*. Edited by Henry de Vocht. Louvain, 1927.

Middleton, Thomas. "The Black Book." In *Works,* edited by Alexander Dyce. vol. 5. London, 1840.

Mirandola, Pico della. "Oration on the Dignity of Man." Translated by Elizabeth L. Forbes. In *The Renaissance Philosophy of Man*. Chicago, 1948.

Mortensen, Johan M., ed. *Le Théâtre français au Moyen Age*. Paris, 1903.

Ockham, William. *Philosophical Writings*. Translated by Philotheus Boehner. New York, 1957.

Ong, Walter J. "Wit and Mystery: A Revaluation in Medieval Latin Hymnody." *Speculum* 2 (July 1947) : 310–41.

Origenes. *On First Principles*. Translated by B. W. Butterworth. London, 1936; reprint ed., 1966.

Patrologia Graeca. Edited J. P. Migne. vol. 29. Paris, 1857.

Patrologia Latina. Edited J. P. Migne. vol. 42. Paris, 1886.

Petit de Julleville, Louis. *Les Mystères*. 2 vols. Paris, 1880.

Phillip, John. *Patient and Meek Grissell*. Edited by W. W. Greg and R. B. McKerrow. Malone Society Reprint. Oxford, 1909.

Potter, Robert. *The English Morality Play*. London, 1975.

Pride of Life. Edited by Alois Brandl. In *Quellen des Weltlichen Dramas in England vor Shakespeare*. Strasbourg, 1898.

Reese, William. *Music in the Middle Ages*. New York, 1958.

Respublica. Edited by L. A. Magnus. Oxford, 1905.

Rossiter, A. P. *English Drama from the Early Times to the Elizabethans*. London, 1950.

Sackville, Thomas. *Mirror for Magistrates*. Edited by Lily B. Campbell. Cambridge, 1938; reprint ed., New York, 1960.

Salinger, L. G. "The Revenger's Tragedy and the Morality Tradition." *Scrutiny* 11 (March 1938) : 402–24.

Schoenbaum, Samuel. "The Revenger's Tragedy: Jacobean Dance

of Death." *Modern Language Quarterly* 15 (September 1954): 201–7.

Select Library of the Nicene and post-Nicene Fathers of the Christian Church. Edited by Philip Schaff. 2d ser. New York, 1895.

Shakespeare, William. *The Tempest.* Edited by Frank Kermode. Cambridge, Mass., 1954.

———. *Henry IV Part 2.* Edited by Norman Holland. New York, 1965.

———. *The Complete Signet Shakespeare.* Edited by Sylvan Barnett. New York, 1972.

Skelton, John. *Magnificence.* Edited by Robert L. Ramsey. Oxford, 1908.

Smalley, Beryl. *The Study of the Bible in the Middle Ages.* Oxford, 1952.

Song of Roland. Translated by Dorothy Sayers. London, 1957.

Spencer, Theodore. *Death and Elizabethan Tragedy.* Cambridge, Mass., 1936.

Spivack, Bernard. "Falstaff and the Psychomachia." *Shakespeare Quarterly* 9 (1957) : 449–59.

———. *Shakespeare and the Allegory of Evil.* New York, 1958.

Spivack, Charlotte. "Macbeth and Dante's Inferno." *North Dakota Quarterly* 28 (1960) : 50–52.

Sternfeld, Frederic W. *Music in Shakespearean Tragedy.* London, 1963.

Tatlock, J. S. "Medieval Laughter." *Speculum* 21 (July 1946): 289–94.

Thompson, E. N. S. *The English Moral Play.* New Haven, Conn., 1910.

Tourneur, Cyril. *The Revenger's Tragedy.* Edited by R. A. Foakes. London, 1966.

Towneley Plays. Edited by George England and A. W. Pollard. London, 1897.

Trial of Treasure. Edited by J. O. Halliwell. Percy Society vol. 18. London, 1850.

Wager, Lewis. *Life and Repentance of Mary Magdalene.* Edited by F. I. Carpenter. Chicago, 1902.

Wager, W. *Enough Is As Good as a Feast.* Edited by Mark Benbow. Lincoln, Neb., 1967.

Wapull, George. *The Tide Tarrieth No Man.* Edited by E. Ruhl *Jahrbuch* 43 (1907).

Wilson, Dover. *The Fortunes of Falstaff.* Cambridge, 1953.

Woodes, Nathaniel. *Conflict of Conscience.* Edited by Herbert Davis and F. P. Wilson. Oxford, 1952.

York Plays. Edited by Lucy Toulmin Smith. Oxford, 1885.

Index